Fundology

The Secrets of Successful Fund Investing

John Chatfeild-Roberts

Hh Harriman House Publishing

HARRIMAN HOUSE LTD

43 Chapel Street
Petersfield
Hampshire
GU32 3DY
GREAT BRITAIN

Tel: +44 (0)1730 233870
Fax: +44 (0)1730 233880
Email: enquiries@harriman-house.com
Website: www.harriman-house.com

First published in Great Britain in 2006
Copyright: John Chatfeild-Roberts and Jupiter Asset Management Limited 2006

Published by Harriman House Ltd
In association with Half Moon Publishing Ltd
The Old Farm, Cuddersdon Road, Horspath, Oxford, OX33 1HZ
Tel: +44 (0)1865 876484
Website: www.intelligent-investor.co.uk

The right of John Chatfeild-Roberts to be identified as the author has been asserted
in accordance with the Copyright, Design and Patents Act 1988.

ISBN: 1-897-59777-0
ISBN 13: 978-1-897597-77-4

British Library Cataloguing in Publication Data
A CIP catalogue record for this book can be obtained from the British Library.

Printed and bound by Cambridge Printing, Shaftesbury Road, Cambridge.

For Doone, Tom and Harry.

About the author

John Chatfeild-Roberts (43) has been analysing and investing in funds professionally for fourteen years. He and his team manage the **Jupiter Merlin** range of funds of funds, for which they have been voted Best Multi-Manager Group of the Year for an unprecedented three years in a row – 2003, 2004 and 2005. After graduating from Durham University in Economics, his early career was spent serving in the Army both in the UK and abroad. Before moving to Jupiter, he ran similar operations for  Lazard Asset Management and Henderson Administration in the 1990s. He is married to Doone. They have two children, Tom (12) and Harry (10), and live in Stilton Cheese country. John spends his spare time with the family walking and riding in the countryside, and in the summer, playing cricket.

Contents

Preface

In 25 years of observing and writing about the UK financial markets, I have often been struck by the almost total absence of good books about the art of investing in funds. There are some consumer guides of variable quality, and a good number of overly simplistic online guides – but until now, nothing of any substance written by a professional fund investor. The contrast with the number of books about stockpicking and trading, of which there are thousands, could not be more marked.

This contrast in treatment is odd. All the evidence I have seen demonstrates that the great majority of those who try their hand at trading and picking their own stocks fail to do as well as they could by investing in a well-picked portfolio of funds. Owning funds is a much safer and more convenient way of investing your money than investing directly in stocks and shares (let alone trading with geared instruments such as spread betting and contracts for difference). Most professional investors use funds to manage their own money.

So it seems strange there is not more help available for those who want to understand how to pick funds well. There is certainly no lack of demand for the end product. With over £300bn invested in the UK funds industry, many investors do understand that funds are indeed a sensible choice. However, the general tone of much comment is negative; the coverage of some aspects of the funds business in the media is adverse, the academic evidence about the performance of the average fund (not that good) is similarly downbeat, and some investors lack trust in the quality of the service they think they might receive from the industry.

It would be unwise to underestimate the scale of this problem. Many of the funds you can buy in the UK are too expensive for the performance that they actually deliver. As the regulators are right to point out, too many funds also are sold on the wrong basis; usually past performance that subsequently fails to repeat. All this helps to explain why investors may be justified in feeling cautious.

But to my mind, it also reinforces the case for investors finding out how to distinguish the good, the bad and the ugly in the funds business. There are some dodgy estate agents and car dealers in the UK, but that does not mean you cannot buy a good house or a good car, if you know how to go about it. So it is with funds. What we all need is a trustworthy, professional guide to help us find the cream of the crop, because the best funds are well worth having.

In the UK, few professionals are better qualified to provide sensible guidance on this matter than John Chatfeild-Roberts, who runs the fund of funds team at Jupiter Asset Management, having previously carried out a similar function at Lazard Asset Management and Henderson Administration. When he agreed to write this book about what he has learnt as a fund investor, I was delighted. Anybody who knows John knows that he is a man of the highest personal and professional integrity – always the first and most important criterion when dealing with a professional of any kind.

After fourteen years running funds of funds, he also knows the unit trust and OEIC business in this country inside out. In this book John describes his thinking and the way that he and his team (Peter Lawery and Algy Smith-Maxwell) go about choosing funds for their six portfolios. You will, I hope, quickly see for yourself the exceptional qualities that have earned him and his team a string of industry awards in recent years. John's success is fundamentally rooted in the timeless qualities of experience, judgement and common sense – the essential ingredients of any successful investment strategy.

Jonathan Davis

Investment columnist, *The Independent*
Founder and editor, Independent Investor
Chairman, Half Moon Publishing Ltd
www.independent-investor.com
Oxford, December 2005

1

Introduction

"The intuitive mind is a sacred gift and the rational mind is a faithful servant. We have created a society that honours the servant and has forgotten the gift."

Albert Einstein

Investment is intrinsically a simple business – buy low, sell high. However there are only a few people who take enough time and trouble to be good at it. Most people are simply not that interested in the financial markets. The first and greatest attraction of investing in funds has always been that it takes away the strain and hassle of having to master the business of investment yourself.

But there are also several other good reasons, in my opinion, why you should take a keen interest in funds – how they work, what they can do for you, and how best to take advantage of what they have to offer. The purpose of this book is to pass on some of the knowledge and experience that I have gained in the past fourteen years as a professional investor whose job is to pick 10-15 of the best funds each year from the 4,000 or so that are on sale in the UK.

The main focus of the book is on unit trusts and open-ended investment companies (popularly known as OEICs, pronounced 'oiks'). Many of the principles and lessons, however, apply equally to other types of fund. The fund industry suffers from a deplorable surfeit of jargon, and all of these terms will be explained in simple language at some point in the pages that follow.

Here is my list of the reasons for owning or taking an interest in funds:

1. The rewards can be impressive. Over the last ten years, the average fund has produced a return of 124.3%, equivalent to 7.38% per annum. This is comfortably better than the 68.3% or 5.34% per annum that you would have received had you left your money in the bank or building society (as measured by the Bank of England base rate, which of course, no one matches consistently).

2. The best performing funds have naturally done even better still. The top performing fund over the past ten years has made a return of 635% – that is to say, it has turned a £10,000 initial investment into £73,565. Any fund in the top 10% of funds by results has produced a return of at least 198% (far better than any index tracker).

3. Funds give you the benefit of access to some of the smartest professional fund managers around. It is true that there are many poor or indifferent funds around as well, and you need to know how to avoid them – but the best of the bunch, as I hope to demonstrate, are very good indeed.

4. Whether we know it or not, most of us already rely heavily on funds for our savings and retirement. If you have an endowment policy, an

3

investment bond, or a personal pension, for example, you will already be an investor in funds. Given how important they are to your financial welfare, you would be well advised to take an interest in how they work.

5. In their wisdom, successive Governments have provided valuable tax incentives for those who invest in funds in a certain way. PEPs and ISAs, as these tax-efficient ways of holding funds are known, allow you to invest up to £7,000 a year in funds without paying any tax on the gains you make.

6. The idea behind funds – that they give you the chance to invest money in the world's financial markets more safely and more efficiently than you could do yourself as an individual investor – is a sound and proven one. It seems perverse not to take advantage of an idea that has proved its worth over nearly 140 years.

7. Although there are many hazards involved in buying and selling funds, which should not be underestimated, many of the best professional investors have all their own money invested in funds (as I and my wife do). Maybe – just maybe – we know something that could be of value to you too.

8. The range of investment opportunities in funds is infinitely greater than it was 30 years ago. Thanks to advances in information technology, it is now possible for UK investors to put their money into an astonishingly wide range of funds, covering almost every country or type of investment that you can imagine.

It is only fair to admit at this point that funds sometimes get a bad press from academics, regulators and media commentators. This is for a number of reasons. The most common criticisms are that unit trusts and OEICs are too expensive, often perform indifferently and are run primarily for the benefit of the managers who run the funds, rather than for those who invest in them.

It would be foolish to deny that there is truth in some of these criticisms. Some investors do have a disappointing experience from investing in funds, but that is primarily because they lack the knowledge and experience to buy the right funds at the right time, not because there is anything wrong with the concept of funds per se. In the pages that follow, I hope to explain how to avoid making these potentially expensive mistakes.

The best and the worst

The best performing fund over the last five years in the UK turned £10,000 into £38,843, a gain of 288.4%, whereas the worst performing one reduced the value of £10,000 to only £2,183, a loss of 78.2%. The first fund would have nearly quadrupled your money in five years, while the second would have lost four fifths of your starting investment!

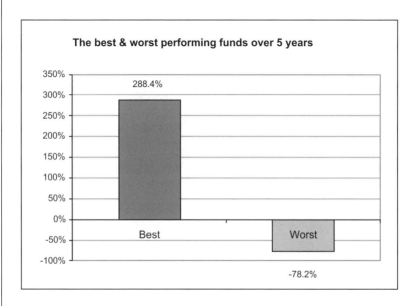

Source: Lipper, to 30th September 2005, Total Return GBP

You would have been very perceptive to have invested in the best fund, and unlucky to have been in the worst. But from these figures you can draw the conclusion that by picking funds with some degree of skill you stand to make good money, whereas if you pick funds with the proverbial pin or without having done sufficient research, you are likely to be disappointed.

The basics of investing in funds

The book is organised in a series of chapters, each one discussing one particular aspect of investing in funds. It does assume some basic knowledge of investment on the reader's behalf. For the benefit of those who are complete novices at investment, I offer here a brief summary of the key concepts in the unit trust and OEIC world. More experienced readers can either skip this section, or use it as a brief refresher course. You may also wish to refer to the glossary at the back of the book.

Unit trusts and OEICs are both examples of what are known as 'open-ended' investment funds. These are investment funds that can grow or contract in size in direct response to investor demand. Like all investment funds, unit trusts and OEICs pool the money of many hundreds or thousands of different investors and hand the investment decision-making over to a professional fund manager employed by the fund management company.

A key principle of both unit trusts and OEICs is that each unit, or share, owned by investors in the fund has an equal status and value to that of any other. Whereas unit trusts operate under trust law, OEICs operate under company law. OEICs are a recent innovation designed to provide a simpler alternative to unit trusts, whose 'dual pricing' structure is sometimes held to be too complicated for ordinary investors to understand.

Unit trusts will always quote investors two prices – an offer, or buying, price and a bid, or selling, price. The first is the price those looking to buy new units will need to pay. The second is the price that those looking to sell their existing holdings will receive. The difference between these two prices is known as the 'bid-offer spread'. As with most financial transactions, the buying price of a unit trust is invariably higher than the selling price. With OEICs, however, investors are quoted a single price at which they can both buy and sell.

Plenty of choice

Funds offer ordinary investors a simple and convenient way to make a wide range of investments in a relatively efficient way. By investing alongside many other investors, fund investors stand to benefit from the advantages of scale and diversification that comes from pooling their money with others. Because of the huge advances in information technology over the past 20 years, the world has literally become the fund investor's oyster, in the sense that the range of available funds now covers all the world's major markets and asset classes.

The drawbacks from investing through funds stem from the fact that there are costs associated with owning funds that can, unless carefully managed, outweigh the potential benefits. At the same time the returns that professional investment managers can make are, in practice, constrained by what the remit of their fund allows them to do with your money. Fund managers with lesser ability find that their efforts can be outweighed by the charges of the fund that they are managing. However, the best fund managers can and do add value consistently, through the exercise of their skill and judgement, over and above the costs.

This existence of below average funds is one reason why passively managed funds (also known as index or tracker funds) have grown in popularity over recent years. Unlike actively managed funds, passively managed funds rely mainly on computer programmes to try and track the performance of specific market indices. Their running costs are typically lower than actively managed funds. Investors today have a choice from scores of different types of fund, including both active and passive funds, in both unit trust and OEIC format.

What you need for success

Because many of those who own unit trusts and OEICs are not very clued up about how to buy and sell their funds in the most effective way, it does create an opportunity for those who know what they are doing to profit. The basic principles are simple and the rewards for those who get it right can be substantial.

As in any other walk of life, one of the secrets of success is not to let yourself fall victim to avoidable mistakes, but to spend a little time educating yourself on how to take advantage of the opportunities available. Investing in funds is no different. Funds are, in the last resort, a known and convenient way to invest your money without much effort – but you do need to know what you are doing before you start.

Give someone a fish, as the old saying goes, and you feed them for a day. Teach them how to fish, and you can feed them for a lifetime. If I can help you understand what to look for when searching for a fund, it will I hope help you to make the most out of a rewarding but often misunderstood sector of the investment business.

The fund concept

"Few people think more than two or three times a year;
I have made an international reputation for myself by
thinking once or twice a week."

George Bernard Shaw

The idea behind funds

The idea of a fund is that it allows someone to invest in a stock or bond market with a small amount of money and little or no expertise. I can do no better than quote the original objective of the world's first investment trust (founded in 1868), as the sentence is applicable to all types of fund or collective investment vehicle. The aim of the trust, reads the document, is: "to provide the investor of moderate means the same advantages as the large capitalists in diminishing the risk of foreign and colonial stocks by spreading the investment over a number of stocks."

This neatly encapsulates the idea of what it is that funds are set up to do for people. That is to reduce the risks of investment by pooling the money of many investors, and then contracting its management out to a professional so as to provide a better return for the investors than they would be able to achieve themselves. The ambition is to provide the benefits available to 'large capitalists' (that is to say, good returns), whilst at the same time reducing the risk by investing in a broad spread of different shares, bonds and other 'stocks'. It sounds a plausible idea; and it is worth looking at more closely.

Diversification and risk

Let us break down the proposition into distinct component parts. Firstly, is the concept of pooling money in order to reduce risk an idea that holds water? What is the risk that is being mitigated? If you look at the risks attached to investing in any single company's shares or bonds, the most serious risk is that the company goes into liquidation or bankruptcy. The risk in that case is that the investor faces losing the entire value of that particular investment.

It is true that investors who own the bonds of a company can often manage to salvage something from the wreckage of a company, although in a process that can take some years. Ordinary shareholders however, those who hold the company's equity (or shares), are the last in the queue of creditors when a company fails and are unlikely to receive a farthing.

Shares and bonds

The owner of a share is a part owner in a company. There are a finite number of shares, which are each of equal value, and which entitle the owner to a pro rata proportion of the distributed profits or dividends. Equity is another term for share.

The owner of a bond is not the part owner of a company. A bond is a debt security, or loan, made to a company (or government), which borrows the money for a defined period of time at a specified interest rate.

The size of company does not necessarily make a difference, as shareholders in Polly Peck found to their cost. When this company went into liquidation in 1990, they all lost their entire investment, even though the company was sufficiently large to be a member of the FTSE 100 Index at the time it failed. (The FTSE 100 Index comprises 100 of the largest companies whose shares are quoted on the London Stock Exchange.)

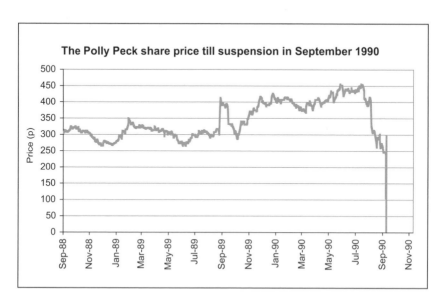

Source: Bloomberg

More recently, shareholders in Marconi, another FTSE 100 company, discovered in 2003 that their investment was worth rather less than they imagined when their company went into administration. The shares, which had been priced at over £12 at their peak in 2000, were eventually converted into 'New Marconi' shares at a value of around 0.8p! The effect of the reconstruction was that shareholders ended up with new shares that were worth just 0.4% of their old ones. To put it another way, they lost 99.6% of their money, top to bottom – essentially a complete loss by any other name.

Source: Lipper

Both examples are salutary reminders that there are real advantages to be had by diversifying your money across the shares of a number of different companies. Diversification, or not putting all your eggs in one basket, is one of the core benefits that you obtain by investing in a fund.

The advantages of scale

But how many companies should you invest in to diversify sufficiently the risk of losing a significant proportion of your wealth? Even expert opinions differ on this matter, but academic theory says that 20-25 different investments would be enough to run a sensibly balanced portfolio. If you own 25 shares with an equal amount in each one, it implies that you will have 4% of your total holdings in each company. If you had £25,000 to invest, that translates into £1,000 per company. This would be all right in theory, but in practice the costs of such an exercise would be too great, quite apart from the time and effort required to research the portfolio and then put it into place.

Most stockbrokers have a minimum commission scale, that is to say they charge the same brokerage fee for any transaction below a minimum size. The charges do not vary much whatever the size of the deal, and although the advent of internet brokerages has meant that more research is available at the click of a button, it still requires time, patience and expertise to trawl through the thousands of companies listed just in the UK, let alone those on overseas markets. Picking your own carefully diversified portfolio of stocks with sums of £25,000 or less is highly unlikely to be a cost-effective exercise, even if you have the time to devote to doing it.

In contrast, the amount of money that professionally managed funds which pool the resources of thousands of different investors have to look after will typically amount to several millions of pounds. In September 2005, according to Lipper, there were 1,857 onshore trusts and OEICs in the UK. The average size of fund was £153m, although that figure does hide a wide divergence. The largest, Fidelity Special Situations, had £5,800m in assets, while the smallest, Singer & Friedlander's Model Portfolio (extraordinarily) was a mere £1,100 in size. However only 59 funds, fewer than 5% of the total, were smaller than £1m in size. The ability to buy stocks and shares in economical quantities is one of the advantages that funds have over you as an individual investor.

In order to make sure that funds are sufficiently well-diversified, there are specific rules that a fund manager must follow which limits the amount of concentration his or her portfolio can have. No one investment can make up more than 10% of the portfolio and the sum of all holdings between 5% and 10% must not add up to more than 40% of the fund. This means that no fund can realistically be run with fewer than seventeen positions. In practice very few have less than thirty investments and many have a list of holdings that stretches into the hundreds. In that sense, diversification is automatically built into the fund concept.

The important point is that the rules governing funds are such that they reduce considerably the risk of complete loss from investment in companies that go 'bust'. Funds are by definition well diversified and have the scale to invest in a cost-effective way. No unit trust in the UK has ever gone bust (though some have lost a lot of their investors' money). Overall therefore, I think that the case for a fund as being an adequate diversifier of the risk of loss of money through company liquidation, or 'absolute risk', is more or less watertight. There are of course many other sorts of risk to which even well diversified funds are exposed, which help to explain why the worst performing fund mentioned earlier lost 78.2% of its value in five years. In general, however, funds are sufficiently diversified to cater for all but the most risk adverse investors.

The returns you can expect

What then about a share of the benefits accruing to 'large capitalists' as the prospectus for the 19th century investment trust put it? It is important at the outset to be clear about what returns are being sought. My view is that investors who put money at risk in fund investments should only do so if they expect to make more money over the longer-term than they can from holding that money in the safest alternative, such as a bank deposit account (known as 'cash' in finance jargon). This is their so-called 'risk-free' alternative.

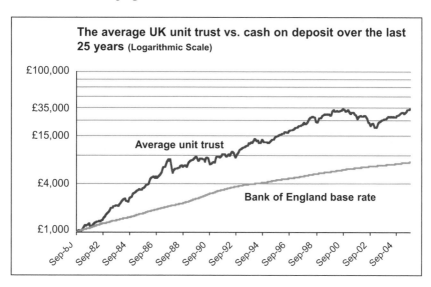

Source: Lipper, £1,000 invested, Total Return GBP, to 30th September 2005

The fact is that over the long run, stock markets do go up. This will continue to be the case as long as economic growth persists since companies, and therefore their shares, grow in tandem with the economy. You may be aware that there are a number of studies showing that shares have generated returns over and above inflation of the order of 6% per annum over the last hundred or so years. A real return of 6% per annum is enough to double the purchasing power of your money every twelve years. At today's inflation rates (around 2.5% per annum), you would need an interest rate of 8.5% to match that kind of return from a bank account or bond.

Of course the long-term, as is often remarked, consists of a lot of short-terms. There is no guarantee that shares will make 6% in real terms over the next three, five or ten years. At different points in time, shares can be cheap or expensive. In the former case, subsequent returns are likely to exceed 6% per annum: in the latter, lower returns could follow. How much money you will make through investing in funds will depend upon the conditions prevailing at the time of the investment, as well as on the skill of the fund manager. The truism that 'a rising tide lifts all boats' is very apt in the world of funds. A stock market that is generally going up (a 'bull market') is likely to make most funds grow, irrespective of the ability of the manager to add value, whereas only the best fund managers will find it possible to make a positive return in a falling (or 'bear') market.

So the question whether funds will provide good returns or not is not clear-cut. The truth is that some will, and some won't. It depends not just on how talented the fund manager is, but on where the fund is investing, and a wide range of other factors as well. Recent experience, as the chart on page 15 shows, has underlined how volatile the stock market can be in the short-term. Share prices on average fell by nearly 50% between 2000 and 2003. This was the worst 'bear market' in living memory; but it followed a period when shares had done exceptionally well, and the market has now recovered very strongly. The trend line is still upward sloping, meaning that those who have the patience to sit out the poor patches will be rewarded in the end.

The majority of funds you can buy are invested in shares and bonds, and the proportion of the fund held in each type of share or bond will have a big bearing on the returns they are capable of generating. The general principle is that the higher the risk, the higher the potential returns investors will expect to make. So for example, a fund that invests in emerging markets will tend to produce higher returns than a fund that invests in a developed market – but the risk of sharp falls along the way is greater.

At the other end of the scale, a money market fund is similar to a bank deposit account – the fund manager looks for the best interest rates in the money markets and pays it out to investors with very little risk to their capital. Bond funds fall into a halfway house between cash and equity funds. They pay a rate of interest, the level of which depends on the riskiness of the bonds they own.

The trick is to identify the best fund managers, work out which conditions they tend to do well in (and when they do badly), invest in their funds at the right time, and finally take your profits at the correct time as well. In short, many people have done considerably better than cash in stock market funds over any reasonable time frame, say five to seven years, and with good judgement, you should expect to do so as well. But although the advertisements don't tell you that timing your entry and exit points is important, trust me; it is.

Points to remember

1. Wherever your money is now, the chances are that a good chunk of it is invested in funds somehow, somewhere.
2. Funds are a proven and effective way of diversifying your holdings and avoiding losses caused by the failure of individual companies.
3. Funds have the advantage of being able to buy stocks and shares in bulk. This is something that individual investors with small portfolios cannot do so cost-effectively themselves.
4. Understanding which conditions will favour a particular fund manager and timing your fund decisions is critical to long-term investment success as a fund investor.

How funds work

"Genius is 1% inspiration and 99% perspiration."

Thomas Edison

This chapter goes into depth on the technical details of unit trusts and OEICs. You may wish to skip this section, and return to it later for clarification if you need to.

The importance of detail

The concept of funds being a collective vehicle for a multitude of investors to use, each owning their slice of the pie, is a relatively easy one to grasp. Each individual puts a certain amount of money into the fund, and in exchange buys a number of units in the fund (or shares in the case of OEICs) at the price at which they were valued on the day of purchase.

A key principle of the unit trust (and OEIC) concept is that every unit you own has the same value as everyone else's (though the number of units you own will obviously depend on how much money you have to invest). However, the minutiae of how unit trusts work are somewhat more complicated and worth an explanation, not least for the fact that large sums of money have been made and lost out of a detailed knowledge of these things.

It is true that most people become bored very quickly when they find they have to concentrate their minds on what appear to be such dry matters. But a little careful study, whilst it may not make you a fortune, can still save you money. This chapter discusses some of these more detailed points. It is necessary background information before we get on to the more interesting question of how to pick the best funds.

The range of funds in the UK

In the UK, there are four main types of open-ended collective fund. They include: unit trusts, OEICs, unit-linked life funds and unit-linked pension funds. Each type of fund works on the same basic concept, but there are significant differences to trip up the uninformed. All four types of fund are similar in that they are collective investment vehicles for pooling investors' money. They are described as 'open-ended' because the size of the fund rises or falls in line with investors' enthusiasm, or demand, for the fund.

Units and shares

There is a difference in nomenclature between a fund investor's holding in a unit trust and an OEIC. While unit trusts are divided into units, OEICs are divided into shares.

The more money that investors put in, or the more investors that it attracts, the bigger the fund can become – the fund manager simply issues more units in order to meet the demand. In the same way, if investors want to pull their money out of an open-ended fund, they can do so simply by selling their units back to the fund provider. The price they receive will be based on their share of the fund's assets at that point. If more investors want to sell than buy, the size of the fund will gradually shrink. If more want to buy than sell, the fund will expand in size to accommodate them.

By contrast, closed-end funds, such as investment trusts, have a fixed number of shares and it is the price that changes in response to investor demand, not the volume of shares or units in issue. The only way to buy into an established closed-end fund on a day to day basis is to buy someone else's shares from them. To sell your shares, you will only be paid the price that someone else is prepared to pay for them – which may or may not be the same as your share of the fund's assets.

One of the reasons why open-ended funds such as unit trusts and OEICs have overtaken closed-end funds in popularity over the last 75 years, despite their apparently higher charges, is that they have proved to be a more flexible way of owning investments. Closed-end funds do not have the same flexibility to increase the number of shares in the fund to meet demand. While in this book I concentrate on the first two fund types, unit trusts and OEICs, the basic principles apply to all four of the open-ended structures I mentioned earlier.

Unit trusts in more detail

Unit trusts were the original open-ended collective investment vehicle for the public in the UK, created in 1931, 63 years after the first investment trust was formed. They are formed under UK trust law, a fact that sets them apart from funds both on the Continent and in the United States. As a legal entity a unit trust is a trust, set up using a trust deed in much the same way that individuals and families often set up trusts or settlements for their heirs and successors.

The trust deed is fundamental to the legal existence of the fund, but is not in my experience a document that is regularly perused by investors. This is despite the fact that it is available for inspection by any investor, and is legally binding on each and every unit holder just as if they had been a party to it. It is signed by the 'manager' and the 'trustee', two key parties in the unit trust world.

The manager of a unit trust is the unit trust company that has set up the fund. The trustee is the guardian of the fund's assets, and in law a distinct entity from the manager. It has the legal responsibility for the safe custody of those assets, as well as collecting any income the fund earns, delivery or taking receipt of any stock that has been sold or bought, and paying any tax due. The trustee also, and crucially, has a general 'duty of care' similar to that which trustees of any kind are given in law.

The scheme particulars

The deed will also refer to a second document, called the Scheme Particulars, which investors would do well to study before deciding whether or not they should invest in a fund. In practice most investors never bother to give it even a cursory glance, but my advice is that they should make a habit of doing so. After a while, you will get used to the legalese, and be able to spot any material departures from normal practice.

JUPITER UNIT TRUST MANAGERS LIMITED

SCHEME PARTICULARS

FOR

Jupiter Merlin Balanced Portfolio

Jupiter Merlin Growth Portfolio

Jupiter Merlin Income Portfolio

Jupiter Merlin Worldwide Portfolio

Valid as at 1 October 2005

JUPITER MERLIN FUNDS OF FUNDS

SCHEME PARTICULARS

Index

Appendices

In the scheme particulars you will find written down the fund's objective, usually couched in bland and general terms (for example, 'to achieve long-term capital growth'), and the investment policy, which defines more precisely what the fund will invest in. This too is still written in broad terms (for instance, a phrase such as 'The fund will invest in Japanese equities').

Here also you will discover the schedule of what the fund will charge investors, and most importantly, the maximum amount that the fund can charge (which is also in the Trust Deed). You should note in passing that a fund need only give 90 days notice of an increase in fees and that increases are not subject to a unit holder vote unless it would take the charge above the maximum level set out in the Deed.

Finally, the scheme particulars will also give details of the administrative arrangements under which the fund will be run. These include the name of the investment adviser (usually a company related to the manager), the trustee, the registrar, the auditors and what their fee arrangements are. It is all undeniably dry stuff, but many organisations make a good living out of this sort of work, so as an informed investor, you should know who they are and seek to understand what they do.

The job of the registrar is to keep the list of unit holders correct and up-to-date, the work usually being undertaken by departments of large institutions. In these days when certificates for shares and units are rarely issued, this is a vital task. In the vast majority of cases unitholders no longer have the security of keeping a certificate, which used to be the legal proof of ownership. Instead, they will have a copy of the entry in the register that lists their name, the latter being the source of the proof.

Over the years in less developed economies, there have been instances of register entries being mysteriously 'rubbed out'! There has been no such occurrence in the UK fund industry, I am happy to say, but the fact that it has happened elsewhere underlines how important the keeping of an accurate register can be.

The legal position of fund investors

The reason for explaining all this at some length is to emphasise that the legal position of a holder of a unit trust is in fact very strong. Specifically, as an owner of units, you are the beneficial owner of your pro-rated share of the fund's investments. To quote a specific Trust Deed: "The scheme property is held on trust by the Trustee for the unitholders in the Scheme, pari passu according to the number of units held by each unit holder."

Pari passu, for those whose Latin is a bit rusty, means that each unit has an exactly equal value and status to any other. Quite how important those words are was demonstrated by the contrasting experience of unitholders and bond holders when the venerable Barings Bank was bankrupted by the rogue trading activities of Nick Leeson in Singapore in the early 1990s (see box).

Barings: a case study

When Barings Bank became insolvent in 1994, people who held accounts or investments with the bank naturally worried how they would be affected by the fallout from Nick Leeson's disastrously unsuccessful trading activities. In the event, investors in Barings unit trusts proved to be in a much stronger position than those who held current accounts at Barings Bank.

Those with bank accounts could have lost most of their money if the bank had not been rescued by the Dutch group ING. Those who had invested in the unsecured bonds Barings had issued did in fact lose all their money. The unit trust owners by contrast were protected from losing their investments by virtue of the fact that their assets were being held for them as beneficial owners by the trustee.

Current account customers at any bank, on the other hand, have their money lent out by the bank many times over, and are dependent on confidence in the banking system for the security of their assets, as many unfortunate customers of Victorian joint stock banks discovered to their cost in the 19th century. The fact that in law unit trusts have an independent trustee is a guarantee of security that investors should not overlook.

OEICs and unit trusts

I have described the functions of the key players in the operation of a unit trust because it is a fundamental principle that you should only invest in what you understand. The same general principles apply to OEICs, but the legal position of this second kind of fund is very different, even if the two types of fund operate in a very similar way.

OEICs were first introduced in the UK in January 1997. They differ from conventional unit trusts in a number of significant ways, most notably in the way that they are priced. An open-ended investment company (OEIC) is, as its name implies, a company that has been set up under corporate rather than trust law. The main difference between an OEIC and a normal company is that an OEIC has a variable capital base, whereas an ordinary company will have a fixed number of shares in issue at any one time.

Unlike a unit trust, an OEIC has no manager, but most of the same functions are discharged by the 'authorised corporate director'. The equivalent of the trustee is the 'depositary', but its functions are limited to custody, the collection of income, the delivery or receipt of stock, and the payment of tax. The duty of care that is placed on the trustee of a unit trust is carried out in the case of an OEIC by its board of directors. OEICs also have an investment adviser, registrar and custodian in the same way as unit trusts do.

The most important practical difference between a unit trust and an OEIC is the way that the price of the fund is calculated and quoted to investors. Whereas the current value of unit trusts is always given in the form of two different prices, one for those looking to sell, and one for those wishing to buy, OEICs have a single pricing system – one price for both buyers and sellers.

It is important to understand the difference between these two approaches, and the reasons for it. While the concepts behind single/dual pricing are not that complicated, experience shows that many investors can easily become a little confused – and that includes unit trust companies themselves (see the box on page 33 for a cautionary tale).

Dual pricing in action

If you look up a unit trust in a newspaper (see page 30), you will see that they are always listed with two prices, a bid (or selling) price and an offer (or buying) price. The dual pricing system is derived from the stock market, where shares have long been bought at a different price from that which they are sold. In other words, you will be quoted one price for a share if you are looking to buy (the offer price) and a second price (the bid price) if you are looking to sell.

The difference between the two prices is known as the 'spread' or 'turn' that the market-maker takes as a reward for providing the liquidity that enables the stock market to function. Liquidity is a measure of how easy it is to buy and sell shares. Just as shops hold stock to enable shoppers to be able to buy the goods they can see in the windows, so market traders hold stocks of shares and bonds so as to be able to satisfy day-to-day fluctuations in demand.

This is still true of all stock and bond markets today, with the size of spread being a function of the depth of liquidity in each particular share. For example, the spread on most FTSE 100 shares today is of the order of 0.1%–0.2%, whereas for many smaller companies it could be between 3% and 5% for deals of any significant size.

So how does this translate into the prices of a dual priced unit trust? When the creators of the first unit trust offered their new product, they opted to use a similar system, though with slightly different terminology. It is easier to look at a diagram first to see how the different prices of a unit trust relate to each other:

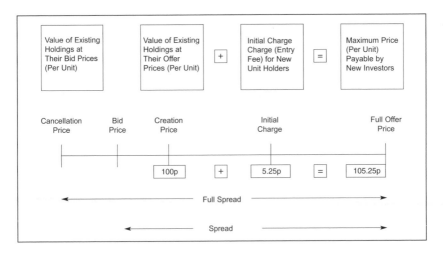

TERMS	DEFINITION
Creation Price	The actual cost of creating new units.
Cancellation (or True Bid) Price	The lowest price that an investor can receive on selling units back to the manager. This is when the fund is on a 'bid basis'.
Bid Price	The selling price that most investors receive when selling units back to the manager. This is when the fund is on an 'offer basis'.
Full Offer Price	The cost of new units to an investor, including the full initial charge, when the fund is on an 'offer basis'.
Bid basis	The pricing basis of a unit trust when there are more sellers of the fund than buyers.
Offer basis	The pricing basis of a unit trust when there are more buyers of the fund than sellers.

What buyers pay

The creation price is the price at which the fund is able to create new units without diluting the interests of existing unitholders. It is therefore the basis for the price you pay to buy units in a fund. It is calculated by adding up the value of all the shares and bonds held in the portfolio, plus any cash in the bank, and dividing the total by the number of units in issue. The holdings are valued at their current market price, using the offer prices quoted by the market-makers for those holdings. For funds investing in the UK, stamp duty, a tax on share purchases, is also included at its current rate (0.5% today).

The price is usually set once a day, often at midday (although more frequent valuation points are possible). It is based on the calculation of the fund's value at that time. As you can place orders to buy or sell units at any time of the day, when investors place their order, it means they always do so without knowing what the exact price will be of the units that they are buying or selling. The price they obtain is the one that prevails at the next valuation point, which may be the following day.

The 'full offer' price is calculated by adding the fund's initial charge (typically 5.25%) to the creation price. This then becomes the price that investors wanting to buy will be quoted. You can confirm this yourself, using a calculator. Multiplying a creation price of, say 100p, by 1.0525 (in the case of a 5.25% initial charge) means that the unit trust would have a full offer price of 100p x 1.0525 = 105.25p.

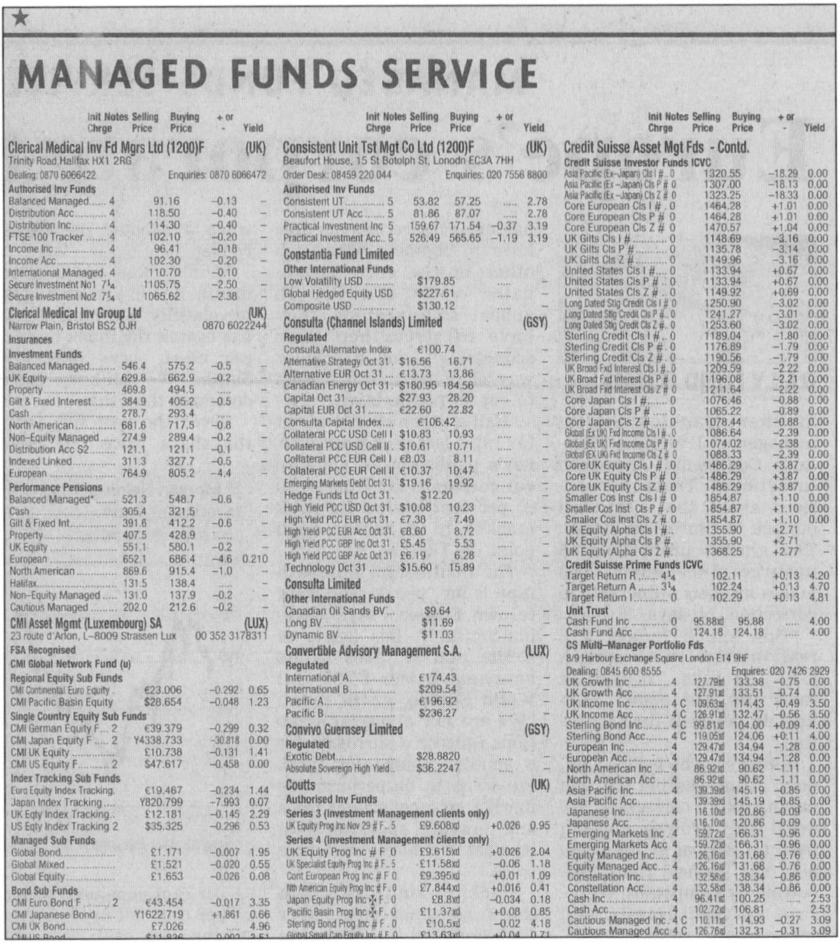

MANAGED FUNDS SERVICE

	Init Notes Chrge	Selling Price	Buying Price	+ or -	Yield
Clerical Medical Inv Fd Mgrs Ltd (1200)F (UK)					
Trinity Road,Halifax HX1 2RG					
Dealing: 0870 6066422 Enquiries: 0870 6066472					
Authorised Inv Funds					
Balanced Managed......	4	91.16		–0.13	–
Distribution Acc..........	4	118.50		–0.40	–
Distribution Inc..........	4	114.30		–0.40	–
FTSE 100 Tracker	4	102.10		–0.20	–
Income Inc	4	96.41		–0.18	–
Income Acc	4	102.30		–0.20	–
International Managed.	4	110.70		–0.10	–
Secure Investment No1	7¼	1105.75		–2.50	–
Secure Investment No2	7¼	1065.62		–2.38	–
Clerical Medical Inv Group Ltd (UK)					
Narrow Plain, Bristol BS2 0JH 0870 6022244					
Insurances					
Investment Funds					
Balanced Managed.........		546.4	575.2	–0.5	–
UK Equity		629.8	662.9	–0.2	–
Property.......................		469.8	494.5	.....	–
Gilt & Fixed Interest........		384.9	405.2	–0.5	–
Cash		278.7	293.4	.....	–
North American.............		681.6	717.5	–0.8	–
Non–Equity Managed		274.9	289.4	–0.2	–
Distribution Acc S2.........		121.1	121.1	–0.1	–
Indexed Linked..............		311.3	327.7	–0.5	–
European		764.9	805.2	–4.4	–
Performance Pensions					
Balanced Managed*		521.3	548.7	–0.6	–
Cash		305.4	321.5	.....	–
Gilt & Fixed Int...............		391.6	412.2	–0.6	–
Property........................		407.5	428.9	.....	–
UK Equity		551.1	580.1	–0.2	–
European		652.1	686.4	–4.6	0.210
North American.............		869.6	915.4	–1.0	–
Halifax..........................		131.5	138.4	.....	–
Non–Equity Managed		131.0	137.9	–0.2	–
Cautious Managed		202.0	212.6	–0.2	–
CMI Asset Mgmt (Luxembourg) SA (LUX)					
23 route d'Arlon, L–8009 Strassen Lux 00 352 3178311					
FSA Recognised					
CMI Global Network Fund (u)					
Regional Equity Sub Funds					
CMI Continental Euro Equity .		€23.006		–0.292	0.65
CMI Pacific Basin Equity		$28.654		–0.048	1.23
Single Country Equity Sub Funds					
CMI German Equity F...	2	€39.379		–0.299	0.32
CMI Japan Equity F	2	Y4338.733		-30.818	0.00
CMI UK Equity		£10.738		–0.131	1.41
CMI US Equity F..........	2	$47.617		–0.458	0.00
Index Tracking Sub Funds					
Euro Equity Index Tracking.		€19.467		–0.234	1.44
Japan Index Tracking....		Y820.799		-7.993	0.07
UK Eqty Index Tracking..		£12.181		–0.145	2.29
US Eqty Index Tracking	2	$35.325		–0.296	0.53
Managed Sub Funds					
Global Bond.................		£1.171		–0.007	1.95
Global Mixed.................		£1.521		–0.020	0.55
Global Equity.................		£1.653		–0.026	0.08
Bond Sub Funds					
CMI Euro Bond F	2	€43.454		–0.017	3.35
CMI Japanese Bond		Y1622.719		+1.861	0.66
CMI UK Bond................		£7.026		.....	4.96
CMI US Bond		[illegible]		[illegible]	[illegible]
Consistent Unit Tst Mgt Co Ltd (1200)F (UK)					
Beaufort House, 15 St Botolph St, Lonodn EC3A 7HH					
Order Desk: 08459 220 044 Enquiries: 020 7556 8800					
Authorised Inv Funds					
Consistent UT..............	5	53.82	57.25	.....	2.78
Consistent UT Acc	5	81.86	87.07	.....	2.78
Practical Investment Inc	5	159.67	171.54	–0.37	3.19
Practical Investment Acc..	5	526.49	565.65	–1.19	3.19
Constantia Fund Limited					
Other International Funds					
Low Volatility USD		$179.85		.....	–
Global Hedged Equity USD		$227.61		.....	–
Composite USD		$130.12		.....	–
Consulta (Channel Islands) Limited (GSY)					
Regulated					
Consulta Alternative Index		€100.74		.....	–
Alternative Strategy Oct 31 .		$16.56	16.71	.....	–
Alternative EUR Oct 31 ...		€13.73	13.86	.....	–
Canadian Energy Oct 31 .		$180.95	184.56	.....	–
Capital Oct 31		$27.93	28.20	.....	–
Capital EUR Oct 31		€22.60	22.82	.....	–
Consulta Capital Index....		€106.42		.....	–
Collateral PCC USD Cell I		$10.83	10.93	.....	–
Collateral PCC USD Cell II .		$10.61	10.71	.....	–
Collateral PCC EUR Cell I .		€8.03	8.11	.....	–
Collateral PCC EUR Cell II		€10.37	10.47	.....	–
Emerging Markets Debt Oct 31.		$19.16	19.92	.....	–
Hedge Funds Ltd Oct 31.		$12.20		.....	–
High Yield PCC USD Oct 31 .		$10.08	10.23	.....	–
High Yield PCC EUR Oct 31 .		€7.38	7.49	.....	–
High Yield PCC EUR Acc Oct 31.		€8.60	8.72	.....	–
High Yield PCC GBP Inc Oct 31 .		£5.45	5.53	.....	–
High Yield PCC GBP Acc Oct 31		£6.19	6.28	.....	–
Technology Oct 31		$15.60	15.89	.....	–
Consulta Limited					
Other International Funds					
Canadian Oil Sands BV...		$9.64		.....	–
Long BV		$11.69		.....	–
Dynamic BV		$11.03		.....	–
Convertible Advisory Management S.A. (LUX)					
Regulated					
International A...............		€174.43		.....	–
International B...............		$209.54		.....	–
Pacific A.......................		€196.92		.....	–
Pacific B.......................		$236.27		.....	–
Convivo Guernsey Limited (GSY)					
Regulated					
Exotic Debt.....................		$28.8820		.....	–
Absolute Sovereign High Yield..		$36.2247		.....	–
Coutts (UK)					
Authorised Inv Funds					
Series 3 (Investment Management clients only)					
UK Equity Prog Inc Nov 29 # F..	5	£9.608xd		+0.026	0.95
Series 4 (Investment Management clients only)					
UK Equity Prog Inc # F	0	£9.615xd		+0.026	2.04
UK Specialist Equity Prog Inc # F..	5	£11.58xd		–0.06	1.18
Cont European Prog Inc # F	0	£9.395xd		+0.01	1.09
Nth American Equity Prog Inc # F .	0	£7.844xd		+0.016	0.41
Japan Equity Prog Inc ✠ F..	0	£8.8xd		–0.034	0.18
Pacific Basin Prog Inc ✠ F..	0	£11.37xd		+0.08	0.85
Sterling Bond Prog Inc # F .	0	£10.5xd		–0.02	4.18
Global Small Cap Equity Inc # F	0	£13.63xd		+0.04	0.71
Credit Suisse Asset Mgt Fds - Contd.					
Credit Suisse Investor Funds ICVC					
Asia Pacific (Ex–Japan) Cls I #..	0	1320.55		–18.29	0.00
Asia Pacific (Ex –Japan) Cls P #	0	1307.00		–18.13	0.00
Asia Pacific (Ex –Japan) Cls Z #	0	1323.25		–18.33	0.00
Core European Cls I # .	0	1464.28		+1.01	0.00
Core European Cls P #	0	1464.28		+1.01	0.00
Core European Cls Z #	0	1470.57		+1.04	0.00
UK Gilts Cls I #	0	1148.69		–3.16	0.00
UK Gilts Cls P #	0	1135.78		–3.14	0.00
UK Gilts Cls Z #	0	1149.96		–3.16	0.00
United States Cls I #....	0	1133.94		+0.67	0.00
United States Cls P # ..	0	1133.94		+0.67	0.00
United States Cls Z # ..	0	1149.92		+0.69	0.00
Long Dated Stlg Credit Cls I #	0	1250.90		–3.02	0.00
Long Dated Stlg Credit Cls P #..	0	1241.27		–3.01	0.00
Long Dated Stlg Credit Cls Z #..	0	1253.60		–3.02	0.00
Sterling Credit Cls I # ..	0	1189.04		–1.80	0.00
Sterling Credit Cls P # .	0	1176.89		–1.79	0.00
Sterling Credit Cls Z # .	0	1190.56		–1.79	0.00
UK Broad Fxd Interest Cls I # .	0	1209.59		–2.22	0.00
UK Broad Fxd Interest Cls P #	0	1196.08		–2.21	0.00
UK Broad Fxd Interest Cls Z #	0	1211.64		–2.22	0.00
Core Japan Cls I #.......	0	1076.46		–0.88	0.00
Core Japan Cls P #	0	1065.22		–0.89	0.00
Core Japan Cls Z #	0	1078.44		–0.88	0.00
Global (Ex UK) Fxd Income Cls I # .	0	1086.64		–2.39	0.00
Global (Ex UK) Fxd Income Cls P #	0	1074.02		–2.38	0.00
Global (Ex UK) Fxd Income Cls Z #	0	1088.33		–2.39	0.00
Core UK Equity Cls I # .	0	1486.29		+3.87	0.00
Core UK Equity Cls P #	0	1486.29		+3.87	0.00
Core UK Equity Cls Z #	0	1486.29		+3.87	0.00
Smaller Cos Inst Cls I #	0	1854.87		+1.10	0.00
Smaller Cos Inst Cls P # .	0	1854.87		+1.10	0.00
Smaller Cos Inst Cls Z #	0	1854.87		+1.10	0.00
UK Equity Alpha Cls I #..		1355.90		+2.71	–
UK Equity Alpha Cls P #.		1355.90		+2.71	–
UK Equity Alpha Cls Z #.		1368.25		+2.77	–
Credit Suisse Prime Funds ICVC					
Target Return R	4¼	102.11		+0.13	4.20
Target Return A	3¼	102.24		+0.13	4.70
Target Return I...........	0	102.29		+0.13	4.81
Unit Trust					
Cash Fund Inc	0	95.88xd	95.88	.....	4.00
Cash Fund Acc	0	124.18	124.18	.....	4.00
CS Multi–Manager Portfolio Fds					
8/9 Harbour Exchange Square London E14 9HF					
Dealing: 0845 600 8555 Enquires: 020 7426 2929					
UK Growth Inc	4	127.79xd	133.38	–0.75	0.00
UK Growth Acc	4	127.91xd	133.51	–0.74	0.00
UK Income Inc............	4 C	109.63xd	114.43	–0.49	3.50
UK Income Acc...........	4 C	126.91xd	132.47	–0.56	3.50
Sterling Bond Inc.........	4 C	99.81xd	104.00	+0.09	4.00
Sterling Bond Acc........	4 C	119.05xd	124.06	+0.11	4.00
European Inc	4	129.47xd	134.94	–1.28	0.00
European Acc..............	4	129.47xd	134.94	–1.28	0.00
North American Inc	4	86.92xd	90.62	–1.11	0.00
North American Acc	4	86.92xd	90.62	–1.11	0.00
Asia Pacific Inc...........	4	139.39xd	145.19	–0.85	0.00
Asia Pacific Acc...........	4	139.39xd	145.19	–0.85	0.00
Japanese Inc...............	4	116.10xd	120.86	–0.09	0.00
Japanese Acc..............	4	116.10xd	120.86	–0.09	0.00
Emerging Markets Inc .	4	159.72xd	166.31	–0.96	0.00
Emerging Markets Acc	4	159.72xd	166.31	–0.96	0.00
Equity Managed Inc.....	4	126.16xd	131.68	–0.76	0.00
Equity Managed Acc....	4	126.16xd	131.68	–0.76	0.00
Constellation Inc.........	4	132.58xd	138.34	–0.86	0.00
Constellation Acc........	4	132.58xd	138.34	–0.86	0.00
Cash Inc	4	96.41xd	100.25	.....	2.53
Cash Acc.....................	4	102.72xd	106.81	.....	2.53
Cautious Managed Inc .	4 C	110.11xd	114.93	–0.27	3.09
Cautious Managed Acc	4 C	126.76xd	132.31	–0.31	3.09

Unit trust and OEIC prices are published daily in the Financial Times and regularly in most other newspapers.

What sellers receive

Turning to the bid price, which is the price you will receive if you choose to sell your units, there is also scope for some confusion. The cancellation price, also known as the 'true bid' price, is calculated in the same way as the creation price, except that it takes the bid prices of the underlying shares (what you could actually sell them for) rather than the offer prices (what you could buy them for). Because the buying price of shares, or any financial investment, is always higher than the selling price, so the offer price of unit trusts is invariably higher than the bid price.

Alert readers will have noticed on the diagram on page 28 that there is a second bid price, just to the right of the cancellation price. Why is this? In some cases, such as a fund that invests solely in FTSE 100 shares, the bid price and the true bid price will be approximately the same. However in others, such as funds with smaller companies in their portfolio, where there is a large spread in the underlying shares, the two prices will be wider apart.

In these cases, the bid price quoted by the company offering the fund will be slightly higher than the true bid price. This is because most fund management companies prefer not to offer funds with a spread of more than say 6.0% to 6.5% between their offer and bid prices, thinking that such a large spread could deter investors. In the case of a UK smaller companies fund, the spread between the full offer and the cancellation prices could be as much as 10% if they were calculated in the normal way.

What the manager will do in these cases is to decide on a level for the bid price which it judges to be reasonable, with the important proviso that the price it chooses should not materially dilute other owners. This will be the case as long as the level of redemptions from the fund is small. The company will always reserve the right, however, to move from an offer to a bid basis so as to use the true bid, or cancellation price, if the value of redemption orders received would materially dilute the remaining holders of the fund.

The pricing of OEICs

In the early 1990s, it was felt by some people in the industry that dual pricing was confusing to investors and out of date (and having read the previous section you may agree with them!). This prompted the industry to lobby for the introduction of a new type of fund, known as the OEIC, which has a simpler, single pricing system. After nine years, there are now more OEICs in the UK than there are unit trusts – but whether the new type of fund has proved to be as simple and effective in practice as its proponents hoped is open to question.

An OEIC's price is calculated in a similar way to a unit trust, by adding up the value of all the assets and cash in the portfolio (but this time using the mid-market price) and dividing the total by the number of shares in issue. One consequence is that investors with small sums to invest, if they don't pay an initial charge, may pay less than the 'creation' cost, while those who sell can receive slightly more than the 'bid' price. People dealing at the single price are therefore making a small amount of money at the expense of the fund and diluting existing or remaining shareholders. In ordinary circumstances, the effect on the fund is not material, and most OEICs charge what is called a 'dilution levy' to stop large deals (which would have a material effect) diluting the interests of other shareholders.

More recently, some companies have been changing the way their OEIC prices are calculated to use what is called a 'swinging single price'. This has the same effect as dual pricing, in that the price of the fund can be moved, within certain limits, known as a 'tunnel', to stop large buyers or sellers diluting the fund at the expense of others. It can lead to fluctuations in the daily price of an OEIC which cannot be explained just by moves in the market. Only the most attentive investors will notice. The justification is that it does protect the interests of remaining shareholders, but it undoubtedly represents a dent in the supposedly superior method of single pricing.

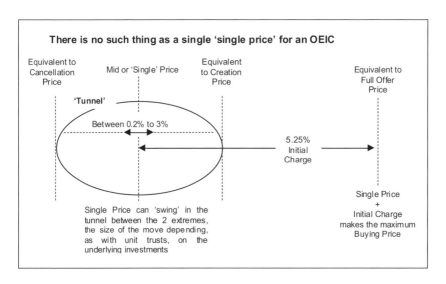

Is single pricing actually better? My view, for what it is worth, is that consumers should be treated as educated adults, and that therefore it should not be necessary to use 'smoke and mirrors' in this way to make funds more palatable. Dual pricing has my vote. However there is no doubt that single pricing has the advantage of being somewhat less confusing to the casual investor.

Even professionals can slip up

In the early part of the 21st century, a well known fund management company launched some new funds of funds, that is to say funds that invest in other funds. They created them as single priced OEICs, but invested their assets in a combination of OEICs and unit trusts. They used the single price of the OEICs and the mid-price of the unit trusts to calculate their own daily single price. All seemed set fair. The performance was above average, the funds were heavily advertised and money started to roll in from investors.

All was well until the auditors appeared for the first statutory annual audit. What they found was that the method of pricing the fund management company had adopted left something to be desired. The particular problem was the way the mid-price on the unit trusts had been calculated. The true mid-price of a unit trust is (logically enough) the mid-way point between the cancellation and creation prices. Unfortunately (and you might think unbelievably) in the case of this particular fund management company, it had decided to use a mid-price half way between the full offer and bid prices, a result that can be shown thus:

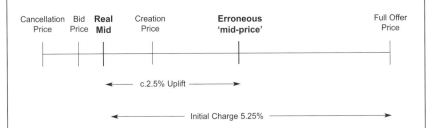

As you can see, if they were buying their units at creation price, which as an institution they would be able to, those same units were then put into the funds of funds with an immediate uplift of around 2%, thus artificially increasing their own OEIC's price.

The knock-on effects of this simple error were enormous. It meant that the performance of the funds involved had been systematically overstated for more than a year. Instead of being well above average performers, calculating their records on the correct basis showed them to be very little better than average. The performance figures had to be recalculated for every single one of the 300 or so days that the fund had been priced incorrectly.

It also meant that every shareholder who had bought the fund after its initial launch had paid too high a price for their units. The annual management fees (what the management company received for its efforts), were also larger than they should have been if the correct figures were used. In fact, the combined costs of this simple error in calculating the prices of the fund are estimated to have added up to around £2m!

To be fair to the company concerned, it paid up with alacrity so that nobody was left out of pocket. Those who had gained from the situation were not asked for the extra money back. The fund industry, I think, comes out well of the episode. It is a good rule in business that if you make a mistake, you should hold your hand up to admit the mistake, and reimburse people fairly and promptly. If you do that, they will probably become your best customers.

What the episode shows, however, is how important attention to detail is and why it is important to take the trouble to understand exactly how the prices of funds work.

Points to remember

1. All investment funds pool the money of many different individual investors and invest it professionally, to gain the advantages of scale.

2. Unit trusts and OEICs are both types of open-ended funds; that is, they expand or contract in size in response to demand.

3. Unit trusts employ a dual pricing system, with one price for buyers and another for sellers. OEICs use a single price for both buyers and sellers.

4. The legal position of unit trusts and OEICs is very strong – investors' money is ring-fenced against losses elsewhere, unlike current accounts.

5. It pays to understand the mechanics of how fund prices are set. Even professionals can make mistakes in this area.

4

Growth or income, or both?

"A gambler is someone who plays slot machines. I prefer to own slot machines."

Donald Trump

General principles

The British Army, and probably most business schools, teach the dictum that before embarking on a project or task, you must first define your aim or objective. In fact, they go further by saying that you are not allowed to have multiple objectives. You should instead set yourself a single overriding aim, and then a number of subsidiary aims. The idea is to have clarity of thought.

The principle holds good for the world of investment. Many people only have a woolly notion of what their financial needs may be in the future; it is only a small minority who put serious thought into what their financial game plan should be. I would hazard a guess that there is one common feature of the human race when it comes to money; however much money you may have, most people will think that they need a little bit more.

As Nelson Rockefeller once memorably said: "How much is enough?" And of course, the point of investment is to try to make money grow, so that by forgoing its use today, you will have more to spend tomorrow. It follows that investment is about taking on (slightly) more risk than that you incur by leaving money on deposit at the bank in order to earn a better return.

There are many textbooks about what sort of investment strategy you should employ, but my feeling is that there is a great deal to be said for straightforward thinking and common sense rather than financial wizardry. Everyone starts from a different initial position. You may have a large capital sum to invest as a private individual, you may be the trustee of a pension fund or charity, or you might be trying to build up a capital sum for your retirement or for a specific purpose such as school fees.

Within those broad outlines, there will also be subdivisions. You might have had (say) an inheritance, have no need of the capital or any income for the moment, but you will want to take an income in the future. On the other hand, you may have urgent need of an immediate income from that capital, to the extent that you are prepared to see the capital sum diminish over time. Whichever it is, make sure that you know what it is that you want and what you can realistically hope to achieve, rather than looking through rose-tinted spectacles and trusting to luck.

There are many examples over the years of people investing in 'get rich quick' schemes that purported to offer significantly above average returns for little or no risk. In almost all cases, the investors lost all their money. The moral is: don't be a sucker. It cannot be said too often that if an investment proposition sounds too good to be true, it usually is.

Income or growth?

So which is it to be: income or growth? Another way of putting this might be: "can you have your cake and eat it?" In general, the majority of private investors want to have an income from the outset. For fund managers, this is an inhibiting requirement as it reduces the pool of potential investments, as well as limiting their freedom of action. For the investor, the instinctive human desire is to have the maximum income possible on day one. It is only common sense however to say that, in the quest for a rising income over time, you should accept that part of the trade-off is a lower level of dividend income initially.

At the time of writing (October 2005), UK base rates are at 4.5% and the FTSE All Share Index yields exactly 3% net to a basic rate taxpayer (thanks to a tax system introduced by the current Chancellor of the Exchequer, Gordon Brown). There are some, though not many, deposit accounts available that pay a gross rate of interest of 4.50%. This is equivalent to 3.60% after tax for someone who pays basic rate income tax. In other words, someone who invests £10,000 in a bank deposit account will receive £360 a year in interest income. An equivalent investment in the stock market would produce a dividend income of £300 in the first year. If interest rates were to stay at the same level indefinitely (which I think is unlikely; they will probably fall), you can work out that the overall dividend payout only needs to rise by around twenty percent to match the deposit interest rate. How long will that take?

If we make the assumption that dividends will grow at the rate of 5% per annum (which would not be an unreasonable assumption), it takes just four years for the dividend level to rise the required 20% to match the initial deposit account interest payments. Furthermore, all things being equal, the capital value of the fund should have risen roughly in line with its income producing ability. From these figures, you might reasonably say that UK shares are not expensive compared to the level of interest rates.

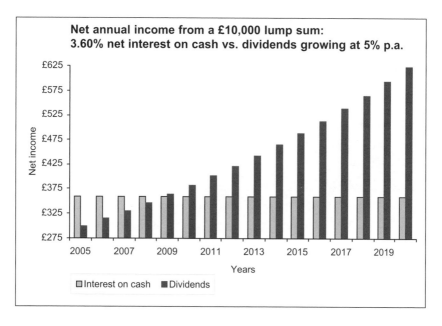

Source: John Chatfeild-Roberts

The widow's tale

In the early years of my career, I came across the very sad story of an old lady who lost a great deal of money. She owned a large house with a reasonable amount of land, and was very concerned about the potential effects of death duties on her ability to pass on these assets to her children. Unfortunately (this was in the days before financial advisers were regulated), she fell victim to some appalling financial advice, the purpose of which was to try to make her assets work "twice as hard" as before, in a misguided attempt to avoid the inheritance tax liability.

What she was persuaded to do was to borrow a large amount of money against the security of her property. The loan was in Swiss francs, which at that time could be borrowed at a considerably lower rate of interest than sterling. She was then told to turn the proceeds into sterling and invest the money in the UK stock market.

Unfortunately two things then happened. First, the Swiss franc went up in value against almost all other currencies, particularly sterling, and then the 1987 crash happened, when most stock markets across the world fell around 30% in the course of two or three days. The effect of the rise in the Swiss currency was to increase the size of both the loan and the interest payments in sterling terms, whilst the portfolio of UK shares fell sharply because of the crash.

To cut a long story short, after six years, much of this lady's property, as well as the portfolio of funds, had to be sold in order to pay back the loan, which was continuing to increase in size (thanks to the power of compound interest), and there was rather less to hand on to the next generation. This was a sad result that stemmed from some very muddled thinking. In order to make her assets work harder, driven by the desire to avoid inheritance tax, the old lady was in effect made to take on extra financial risk, something she had no need to do. It all could have been avoided if basic principles of prudent financial management had been adhered to.

Inflation and retirement

If the average individual retires at 65 years old, current actuarial tables, taken from the Government Actuaries Department, suggest that they will live to around 83 (84.7 for women, 81.8 for men), or to put it another way, for a further 18 years. The received wisdom of the financial services industry, supported by the regulator, is that investors of such an age should have very little in equity-linked investment and most of their money in fixed interest funds. The reason given is that fixed interest investments are 'safer', by which is usually meant less volatile.

I disagree with this kind of reasoning, as it overlooks the potentially corrosive effect of inflation on the cost of living. While inflation, as measured by such indices as the RPI or CPI, currently runs at around 2-3% per annum, I believe that true inflation, particularly for pensioners, is higher. The prices of goods that are falling, such as electronic goods, mostly made in China, are not in the main those that pensioners need or have much demand for. Yet if you look at what is happening to the price of non-discretionary items, such as council tax, which has risen by roughly 10% per annum for the last eight years, you can see what I mean.

Even if I am wrong, and inflation stays at just 2.5% per annum, after 18 years of retirement, the real cost of £100 worth of expenditure will have risen to £156. Looked at another way, the hapless pensioner trying to survive on a fixed income will have taken an effective 'pay cut' of 36% thanks to inflation. Such would be the result of investing completely in either fixed interest investments, or leaving the money on deposit. The income level cannot go up (unless interest rates soar, which is unlikely) and the net result is a gradual erosion of living standards.

Equity based funds paying an income from dividends can, however, do rather better. Dividends are likely to rise by around 8% this year (2006). They have risen by 5.6% per annum over the last 20 years, and by 8.1% per annum over the last 30 (even allowing for the 1997 'raid' by Gordon Brown, which reduced dividends in that year by a massive 14.4%). It does not take the brains of a rocket scientist to work out that in exchange for some capital volatility, an individual or organization that needs income is almost certainly better off, over any meaningful time frame, being invested in dividend-paying equities than cash or fixed interest. I would describe the above effect as 'getting rich slowly' to ape a recent financial advertisement, or 'value investing' to use fund management jargon.

Capital appreciation has attractions too

On the other hand, there is merit also in investing purely for capital growth. Going back to first principles, in essence an equity or share is valuable because it entitles the investor to a stream of future earnings, discounted by an interest rate. It is certainly a tenable proposition to invest in a company in the hope that it will grow faster than the average, and hence produce swiftly rising earnings. Even if these increased earnings are not paid out as dividends, the shares can still become more valuable.

The rewards can be attractive. For instance, if you had invested $100 in Microsoft's stock at its flotation in March 1986, by February 2003 the value of those shares would have risen 250-fold to over $25,000. Microsoft grew very strongly over those seventeen years, as any observer of what has happened in computing can see. In all that time though, Microsoft did not pay out any dividends, preferring to use the large amounts of cash generated by its operations to reinvest in its own business. More recently it has started to pay dividends as its business matures. The US tax environment has also started to favour companies that pay out dividends. So perhaps Microsoft is no longer a 'growth' company.

Value and growth investing

There is an important difference between 'value' and 'growth' investing. Value investors like to buy shares they believe are cheaper than they are intrinsically worth. They are often prepared to wait a long time for the market to come round to their way of thinking (and sometimes it never does).

Growth investors in contrast buy shares in companies that are growing strongly and which they hope or believe can continue to grow faster than the market expects. If they get it right, they hit the jackpot. More often they have to be hardened to disappointments as growth fails to materialise.

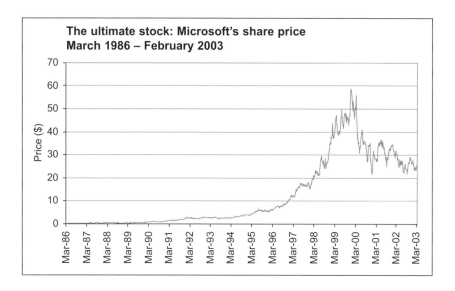

The ultimate stock: Microsoft's share price March 1986 – February 2003

Source: Bloomberg

The trouble with using Microsoft as an example is that it is such an exceptional example. There are any number of companies in the world of computing that started out with the same high hopes but failed to live up to expectations. The same can be said of any industry or sector. Some succeed but in a much smaller way, some are taken over and many go into liquidation. It takes a special skill and a decent amount of luck to find good growth companies. In this sort of investing it is particularly important not to put all your eggs into the one basket. Fund managers in this field can have considerable advantages over a private investor, particularly in access to timely information.

Timeless truths

There are certain immutable 'laws' of investment amongst which the following are worth paying attention to.

1. Periods of financial dislocation, such as the Russian default crisis of 1998 when the Russian Government suspended interest payments on its debt, can create opportunities for those who have spare cash to invest, as long as the worst fears of market participants are not realised. As the saying goes: "Invest when there is blood on the streets."

2. Borrowing to buy financial assets ('gearing') enables you to make profits with the bank's money in rising markets, assuming that the rise is more than the rate of interest charged, but can be very dangerous in markets that fall very quickly. Gearing is what destroyed people in the Wall Street Crash of 1929. Never borrow that which you cannot afford to pay back from other assets.

3. Investments that have no time limit (which includes most funds and shares) are usually safer than those that require something to happen by a certain date. Time will very often bail out a bad investment decision, or one which is right but too early, however, if there is a time limit on an investment, the holder of that investment doesn't have the luxury of being able to wait until the situation recovers. In fact they may find that they are forced out of their investment at the very worst moment. The holders of so-called 'precipice bonds' found this to their cost in the 2000-2003 bear market when they were forced to realise their investments before markets had recovered sufficiently to offset their losses.

4. The long-term is made up of a lot of short-terms. The investment industry advertises, and is required to do so by the regulator, that investment in funds is something that should not be considered for anything less than five years. Yet there are often occasions, when something is going wrong, that prompt action would save money. Selling a technology fund at any time in 2000, for example, would have saved an investor from considerable further losses.

5. It is said that it is "never wrong to take a profit"; and how many 'millionaires' did you know in the spring of 2000 who never did take their profits? However, when you have investments with good fund managers, it is often wrong to take money away from them. Warren Buffett has described taking profits and "rebalancing" (that is adding the money to underperforming investments) as "gardening by digging up the flowers and watering the weeds".

As a final point, it is rare to find individuals who trumpet their investment failures rather than their successes. You tend only to hear about the ones that doubled or more! But as an investor, you must be honest with yourself, particularly in the field of performance measurement. You must include all the duds as well in your calculations in order to compare yourself fairly against either an index or a fund. When you do, you will find that the best professionals are extremely hard to beat. In the property world it is often said that there are three important things to consider when buying a house: 'Location, location and location.' In the world of funds there are also three important factors that you should investigate before you buy a fund: 'People, people and people.'

Points to remember

1. All investors need to form a clear idea of what their investment objectives are.

2. There are sound reasons for picking either income or capital gain as your primary objective as an investor.

3. Because dividends can grow over time, a portfolio of shares with a lower initial yield than cash may still produce a higher annual income within a few years.

4. Equity-based funds are more likely to produce inflation-beating returns over a period of years.

5. In order to achieve this return, you have to be prepared to live with changes to the value of your capital.

6. It is essential to measure the performance of your investments accurately and honestly.

How to pick the best fund managers

"Few great men would have got past Personnel."

Paul Goodman

Keep it simple

Most professions use jargon, either consciously or subconsciously, which prevents outsiders understanding what they do. The fund management industry is no different to any other in this respect. It also has a tendency to make investment sound more complicated than it needs to be. In particular, much importance is placed today on the use of ever more complicated mathematical or quantitative techniques to make investment decisions.

When it comes to buying funds, I strongly believe that this is the wrong way to go about it. In my experience, it is the people who run funds that make the difference. Obviously there are good fund managers and there are bad ones, as in any walk of life. Just think of your own life. There were good and bad teachers at your school, there will have been good and bad builders who have worked on your house, there are good and bad articles written by good and bad journalists, and so on. Life is a people business.

People are all very different and generalising about fund managers is difficult and fraught with danger. Are there attributes that make a good fund manager? There is no definitive list, but I think one can say with certainty that there is no exam you can take to make you a star fund manager, or even to prove that you are one. Mostly people either have the essential skills built into them or they don't, although exposure to the right principles at an early age can be very helpful in bringing those skills to the fore.

An example of this would be William Littlewood, a former fund manager at my firm Jupiter, now at Artemis, whose father was a highly regarded stockbroker with Rowe & Pitman. (John Littlewood's book 'The Stock Market – 50 years of Capitalism at Work', FT Pitman Publishing 1998, is well worth reading.) William says that his initial interest in investments was stimulated by being with his father (and it is observable that many children like to do what their parents enjoy). He then worked hard on his own initiative to develop the skills, which he put into practice during his successful tenure managing the Jupiter Income unit trust: a classic story of outstanding achievement.

The qualities you need

Despite it being difficult to generalise about what makes a good fund manager, in my experience they often share similar characteristics. They are almost always inquisitive, extremely hard working, and at the same time ultra-competitive. But to have these qualities is not enough. A good fund manager needs a clear head and an ability to think for him or herself. The possession of a university degree does not prove, in my opinion, the possession of these characteristics. Some of the best fund managers I know only attended the 'university of life'. A degree is often merely a useful adjunct that shows you can pass exams, but not a lot else.

The ability to think for yourself is very important. There is a lot of 'noise', that is to say meaningless chatter, in any financial market and it is very easy to let it shape your opinions. In these days of instant electronic communication, the risk of information overload is ever present. The best managers use their brains to think about what is going on, read what is relevant, ignoring what isn't, and come to their own conclusions about what they should do next. They do not follow the herd.

If in time they see that they were wrong in a particular instance, they have the humility and psychological honesty to admit their mistake, and to do something about it, even if this means completely reversing direction, taking aggressive, ruthless action to get rid of what is hurting the portfolio, before moving on. This last feature of a good fund manager is probably the most important of all. While we all make mistakes, the key is to make sure that those mistakes harm the performance of the fund as little as possible.

Learning from experience

In the early years of my fund management career, I had the good fortune to come across James Findlay, who at the time worked for Foreign & Colonial, running US smaller company monies for them. Having started in fund management in the early 1980s, he had run F&C's US Smaller Companies unit trust during the October 1987 crash, and had seen what a severe market correction could do to stocks which were 'all hype and no hope'. He set to work re-educating himself in fund management, and came up with a written investment philosophy which he decided he would adhere to from then on.

It could be summarised as following in the value investment tradition of Benjamin Graham and Warren Buffett. He has been astoundingly successful at putting it into practice. (If you are interested in reading more about his investment approach, it is available at www.FindlayPark.co.uk.) Since early 1988 the funds he has run, Foreign & Colonial's US Smaller Companies fund until 1997, and Findlay Park US Smaller Companies fund (since March 1998) have produced staggering performances, as shown in the chart.

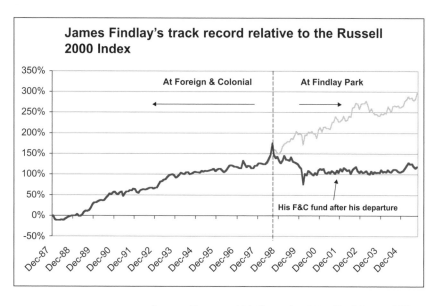

Source: Lipper, to 30th September 2005, Total Return GBP

My team has had the good fortune to have invested our clients' money continuously in James' funds since 1992. The clients have benefited hugely as a result. His fund is closed to new investors, which means that one of the few ways a new investor can access his and his team's unique talents is by buying a fund of funds that already owns a slice of his fund. This includes my own team's Jupiter Merlin portfolios, three of which own the fund.

Finding the best

Given that it is people who ultimately make the difference, how does the investor go about finding the talented few fund managers worthy of support? It is certainly no use saying that you must interview the managers before committing money to them. That will not be a practical option for most private individuals. The best fund managers do not unfortunately have the time to see private investors individually, though teams such as ours with large funds to invest insist on meeting them on a regular basis. If you own investment trusts you can also go to the annual meetings of the trust and talk to the manager on that occasion, but this is not an option with unit trusts or most OEICs.

However reading as much as you can about your target managers, whilst bearing in mind that the marketing or PR department will have had a hand in almost everything that you read, is likely to be helpful. Journalists' output can also be useful, but again remember that not all journalists are equal. When you read anything, including this book, a good rule is that you should always ask yourself: "What is the angle of the person writing this?" Just because something is printed neatly in black and white does not mean to say that it is true.

What I mean by this is that when someone gives you an opinion, you must work out what their vested interest is. Fund managers like to show their performance in the best light and prefer not to talk about their failures for fear of being made to look foolish. And although most journalists are rigorously objective, some may let outside matters colour their judgement, and so on. Again, I don't say this in a critical sense. It is just that life is about people, and people are flesh and blood with all the human frailties that those words imply.

It is also worth looking at what sort of firm an individual works for. Some investment firms have a very regimented style of managing money, which allows little room for individual flair. Others are set up to allow talented individuals the freedom to perform. Some of these firms are very small in size, but it is not always size but attitude of mind that counts. The founders of any firm will usually set the style for how it sets out its stall and investors would be wise to study a firm from this angle. Sir Martyn Arbib who founded Perpetual (now Invesco Perpetual) and John Duffield, who started Jupiter and New Star, both put the emphasis on individual talent, with great success. Good people can do well in a difficult environment, but it is a lot easier if everyone around you has the same ethos.

Fund information

The growth of the World Wide Web has made information about funds easier to come by for private investors and advisers. Some of the sources that you might consider using could be:

- *Citywire (www.citywire.co.uk)*
- *IFAonline (www.IFAOnline.co.uk)*
- *FT Adviser (www.ftadviser.com)*
- *Interactive Investor (www.iii.co.uk)*
- *or the relatively new online TV channel, Asset TV, where you can see fund managers being interviewed (www.assettv-data.co.uk).*

Online newspapers, particularly:

- *The Times (www.timesonline.co.uk)*
- *The Daily Telegraph (www.telegraph.co.uk)*
- *The Independent (http://money.independent.co.uk) also offer plenty of fund information.*

For market data, the business section of the BBC website (http://news.bbc.co.uk/) gives investors most of what one might want to know about markets without a professional Bloomberg connection, and for that matter Bloomberg's website (www.bloomberg.co.uk) is also a good source.

Experience is important

Once armed with this information, what factors should you consider? My view is that experience is worth an awful lot, and many of the best fund managers are the ones who have been investors through both good and bad markets. Remember that investing is as much about being in tune with the psychology of the market as it is about doing fundamental company analysis. It is no good buying shares in a good company at the wrong time. Having experience of how difficult life can be in a prolonged bear market, or (like James Findlay) living through a scary event such as the October 1987 stock market crash, can be of immeasurable help to a fund manager.

However, there are always bright new young men and women coming through. These again are quite difficult for the private investor to spot at an early stage in their careers, but my team make it their business to try and find these rising stars if we can. While experience can be valuable, it is also said that younger, more adventurous fund managers don't suffer from the mental scars of past mistakes, which in turn gives them the confidence to invest in situations that may appear more risky, but turn out in the end to be immensely profitable. In a raging bull market the youngsters can often therefore generate stellar performance; however, on balance I prefer experience over such youthful enthusiasm.

Talking to fund managers

In the final analysis, there is no substitute, we have found, for seeing the whites of someone's eyes. The approach to interviews that my colleagues, Peter Lawery and Algy Smith-Maxwell, and I like to take is organised, but open-minded. We don't go in with 20 pages of questions, as I have seen some firms do, including such fatuous ones as "how many people do you employ in your compliance department?"! We do go in prepared, however, and knowing what we want to find out.

Obviously experience plays an important part in our efforts as well; you don't interview 75 different managers once or twice a year for over ten years without acquiring a large amount of information that we carry around in our heads. The market circumstances of the time dictate what we wish to find out, and when we know someone very well, plenty will be taken as read. For instance there is no need for managers we know well to tell us what their basic approach to the market is. In some ways, the true test of our abilities as 'people-pickers' comes when we are interviewing people we have not met before.

We may see someone as a result of our noticing the good performance of their fund in our regular data-screening exercises, during which we look at the performance of all the funds in our universe (see Chapter Six). Alternatively we may have been given an introduction to a fund manager from someone for whom we have a high regard. In most circumstances, we like to have two of us at a meeting, so that at any point, one of us can be writing and the other looking and thinking. In fact, most interviews, as in other fields besides our own, are something of a game of intellectual poker. It is not so much that a fund manager will have something to hide, rather that, as I have said before, everyone likes to show themselves off in the best possible light, and therefore will be unlikely to highlight their past mistakes and misjudgements.

We, on the other hand, need to find out as much as we can, both good and bad, which involves gently probing and asking *exactly* the right questions in the right way. If you don't ask the right question, you may not find out the vital piece of information that could make the difference between whether you buy a fund or not, or whether you keep it or sell it. One example would be the excitement surrounding the shares of Cairn Energy in 2004. Because the shares of Cairn did so well during that year, almost any fund manager who happened to own the shares would have been able to show good performance as a result.

If you did not know how much Cairn's performance affected returns, it would have been easy to draw the wrong conclusions about a fund manager's skill. The important thing was to find out when the shares were purchased and why, and also how the fund manager handled the situation as the shares kept rising from a low of £3.65 in January to their peak of £15.70 in mid December (they then fell back to £10 in the last two weeks of the year). You would then have to decide whether buying the stock was good luck or good judgement on the part of the fund manager.

It is not necessarily factual answers that we are after. Sometimes we will be interested in their attitude to a share that we know well. Or it could be questions designed to tease out the manager's temperament. However, it is important to keep on good terms with the people you want to manage your money. They are under no obligation to help you if they don't want to, and if they don't like you, they may not want to have you as an investor! Tact and good manners when you are quizzing someone are very important.

Assessing people is an art in itself

One set of factors that I think many people ignore, and yet have a significant effect on personal, and therefore investment, performance are so-called 'soft' factors. These are the pieces of information that when fitted together, create a picture of someone's life. These can range from obvious distractions, such as the state of someone's marriage, or whether there is a career move in the offing, to more nebulous issues, such as how well they sleep on a business trip. On one occasion we chose not to invest in a fund when we discovered quite by chance that the fund manager, who didn't have an assistant or any other backup, commuted to work each day on a large motorbike. It seemed to us that the fund was literally riding on the pillion of his Ducati!

Being a fund manager can be a stressful job too. Not everyone has the constitution to be able to stand the expenditure of nervous energy – and if that is the case, our duty is to know as much. There are very few jobs where your performance can be measured every single day; fund management is one of them and periods of underperformance are there in stark relief for all to see. There is no substitute for seeing the whites of their eyes.

Having started the chapter saying that it is hard to pin down what makes a good fund manager, you can see that in truth it is very hard indeed. However as I get older, throughout my everyday life I find myself subconsciously categorizing people I meet quite quickly, comparing them to similar personalities I have met in the past. I don't know if you find that resonates with you, but I certainly find it helpful in trying to identify whether the fund manager I am interviewing is 'the real thing'.

Essentially, if fund management was purely a science rather than an art, it would be possible to learn how to get the right answer every time. We all know that is just not the case and that there is no one right way of managing money. Otherwise how could people such as Philip Gibbs of Jupiter and Neil

Woodford of Invesco Perpetual succeed in their completely different ways? Similarly, picking fund managers is also an art; there are clues to be found in their performance records, in what they say and in what their portfolios reveal about them, but after all is said and done you have to weigh up the evidence and make a decision, remembering to include a judgement about whether the general conditions will suit them.

There is no table of scores you can create to prove whether you are right or wrong, and some of your judgements will turn out to be wrong. However if you invest with experienced, decisive, clear-headed, competitive and contrarian fund managers and give them enough time to go through the odd bad patch, you will find that the performance of your investment portfolio will improve considerably.

Points to remember

1. Judging people is the best way to pick good fund managers.
2. Good fund managers all share qualities – hard work, competitiveness and curiosity.
3. The best ones also have the ability to think for themselves – and admit they have made mistakes.
4. Young fund managers can often start very impressively, but in the long run, experience counts for more.
5. There is no substitute for seeing how a manager reacts to the inevitable periods of poor performance.

What can past performance tell you?

"Life has no rehearsals, only performances."

Anon

The UK Stock Market Almanac 2006

Facts, figures, analysis and fascinating trivia that every investor should know about the UK stock market

Edited by Stephen Eckett

What is the UK Stock Market Almanac?

The Almanac is an essential companion to guide you through the next financial year and is comprised of several parts. The diary section contains all the day-to-day information you will need, including: futures expiry dates and exchange holidays, a weekly round-up of interims and finals to keep you up-to-date, and a money-related 'on this day' fact for each day of the year. Each week there is an accompanying seasonal article to keep you entertained by highlighting some lesser-known quirks of the market.

The comprehensive reference material is a useful resource for those investment-related questions, and an extensive section devoted to company data will give you a wide range of information on any company listed on the London Stock Exchange.

The Almanac is a unique reference work, its purpose to inform, educate and entertain anyone interested in the UK stock market – a must-have for any serious investor and packed with so much useful information that it is the *only* book you will need on your desk in 2006.

What does the 2006 Almanac have in store?

Again in the Almanac we celebrate the Efficient Market Theory – or rather the failure of said theory. To briefly recap, Efficient Market Theory states that it is impossible to beat the markets, because prices already incorporate all known information. What a dull place the stock market would be if this was really true!

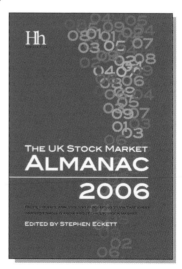

In this edition we look at answering questions such as:

- Which sectors perform best in the first quarter of the year?
- Which is the strongest week for the market in the year?
- Why is September the worst month for the market?
- Which months do mid-caps outperform large caps?
- How do the markets react to the MPC interest rate announcements?
- What's the probability of the market rising 4 months consecutively?
- What happens to stocks that are ejected from the FTSE 100 Index?
- Should investors should buy FTSE 350 Dog Stocks?
- And – the biggest market anomaly of them all – does the six-month phenomenon still exist?

Harriman House
www.harriman-house.com

> "No investor should be without this superb diary on their desk next year."
>
> *Robbie Burns, www.nakedtrader.co.uk*

Sample pages

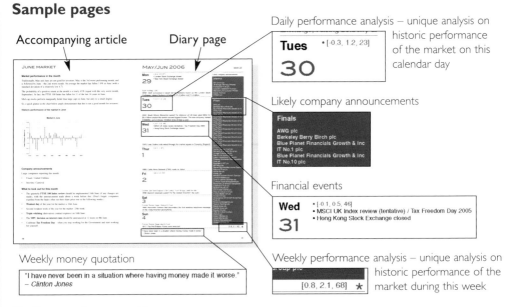

Accompanying article   Diary page

Daily performance analysis – unique analysis on historic performance of the market on this calendar day

Tues • [-0.3, 1.2, 23]

30

Likely company announcements

Finals

AWG plc
Berkeley Berry Birch plc
Blue Planet Financials Growth & Inc
IT No.1 plc
Blue Planet Financials Growth & Inc
IT No.10 plc

Financial events

Wed • [-0.1, 0.5, 46]
• MSCI UK Index review (tentative) / Tax Freedom Day 2005
31 • Hong Kong Stock Exchange closed

Weekly money quotation

"I have never been in a situation where having money made it worse."
– Clinton Jones

Weekly performance analysis – unique analysis on historic performance of the market during this week

[0.8, 2.1, 68] ★

Bulk purchase options

Not only essential to the private investor or trader, the Almanac also makes an excellent corporate product, for distributing either to clients or staff.

We are therefore offering the opportunity to purchase bulk copies of the Almanac at special rates. Harriman House can also manage the mailing out of copies to your clients if required.

For more information please contact:
Claire Wright on 01730 233870
or at cwright@global-investor.com

The purchase rates for orders are as follows:

Order size	Unit price
10-50 copies	£12 per copy
50-100 copies	£10 per copy
100-250 copies	£9 per copy
250-500 copies	£7 per copy
500-1000 copies	£5.50 per copy
1000+ copies	£5 per copy

Ordering information

The UK Stock Market Almanac 2006 (RRP: £19.99) is available to order:

By phone:

+44 (0)1730 233870

By fax:

+44 (0)1730 233880

By email:

bookshop@harriman-house.com

Online:

www.harriman-house.com/almanac

By post:

Harriman House Ltd
43 Chapel Street
Petersfield
Hampshire
GU32 3DY

and from all good bookshops.

Mirror, mirror on the wall

When you look in a mirror, what do you see? You see a reflection of yourself. When you look in your car's mirror, what do you see? With any luck what is behind you. When you look at the past performance of a fund, what do you see? You see what <u>has</u> happened to the fund. What you don't see is what <u>will</u> happen in the future. However if you look carefully, and know where to look, I believe that it is possible to pick up clues as to what might happen next – and that is one of the keys to investing in funds.

When someone buys a fund, on what rational basis do they do so? Do they like the brand of the company and have faith in it? Do they ask for advice from either friends or financial professionals? Do they use some evidence to decide whether it is good or bad? Perhaps they use a combination of all three. However, what evidence is there? In factual terms, there is the level of charges on a fund, and how its manager has done over the years. Are you telling me that you would buy some other service, such as an accountant, blind? I hope not. No, you would ask around, find out who had done a good job for people in the past and perhaps ask for examples of what they had done for other clients. In other words you would look for evidence of their ability through looking at their past performance.

The regulator requires advertisements to say "past performance is no guide to the future", and I would agree with the sentiment, if all you are doing is extrapolating the trend of what has happened into the future ad infinitum. However, as Mark Twain said: "History, although it never repeats itself, often rhymes." By the same token, the past performance of a fund manager can tell you quite a lot about how they invest, and therefore can give you some guide as to what their performance might be like in the future. This will only hold good though, if you look at it in the right way.

Unfortunately however, human nature is such that the vast majority of people do not expect change, but instead believe, consciously or subconsciously, that the current trend will carry on forever. It is a fact that most people prefer to invest in something that is already doing well rather than something that has had a bad time, presumably because it reinforces their confidence in their investment. As a simplistic method of picking investments in funds, I am afraid that it doesn't have much to recommend it. You need to know why a fund (and its manager) has done well or badly. The history of investment is littered with examples of funds that did very well for a time, but which then disappointed investors, most of whom climbed on the bandwagon too late and therefore didn't benefit from the good performance in the early years.

A trail of clues

As I said, my view is that past performance of a fund can give you some clues. How can you use performance records to discover what type of investor someone is, and whether they are good or not? There are several software products on the market, such as that sold by Style Research Associates, which try to do this. In the jargon what they offer is something called 'returns based analysis' (see Glossary).

Firms such as Style Research use sophisticated mathematical modelling techniques to calculate where they think the returns of a fund came from, based purely on the price movement of a fund. The output breaks down each day's return, and gives you a graph over time showing the percentage returns derived from growth stocks, value stocks and so on. It is clever stuff, and gives some pretty output, which is available to individual investors at www.styleresearch.co.uk/ora/int/introduction.aspx. However, it has great limitations, not least in the choice of underlying return components that it uses (it calls them paradigms), but it does give relative performance graphs over the last ten years, so that you can see if apparent good performance is the result of a 'one-hit wonder'.

Another way professionals analyse past performance is to use portfolio analysis software. This is available from a number of different providers, the best known being BARRA (see opposite). What the software does is study, in detail, the characteristics of the stocks that are held in a fund's portfolio at a particular point in time. This tells you a wealth of information; amongst other things, whether the fund you are looking at is targeting small, mid or large cap stocks, or some combination thereof. It tells you what the sector 'exposures' of the fund are; that is, how much of the portfolio is in each segment of the stock market – how much in banks, how much in oil companies and so on. It will show you the 'riskiness' of the fund as measured by its 'tracking error', the extent to which its return may deviate from the market as a whole. It will also show whether the fund has a 'growth' or a 'value' bias.

Example of BARRA output

RISK DECOMPOSITION	Risk (% Std Dev)	Contribution (% Active Risk)
Risk Indices	4.82	76.06
Industries	1.84	11.06
Covariance * 2	N/A	1.99
Asset Selection	1.82	10.89
Active	5.53	
Benchmark	10.85	
Total	12.55	

RISK INDEX EXPOSURES	Managed	Benchmark	Relative
Size	-0.82	0.02	-0.84
Momentum	0.25	-0.01	0.26
Volatility	0.49	0	0.5
Trading Activity	0.09	0.01	0.07
Leverage	-0.17	0.01	-0.18
Value	-0.14	0	-0.15
Yield Ri	-0.54	0.01	-0.55
Foreign Sensitivity	-0.21	0.01	-0.22
Growth	0.33	-0.01	0.34
Midcap	0.25	0.14	0.11
Non-Fta Indicator	0.12	0	0.12

INDUSTRY-SECTOR EXPOSURES	Managed	Benchmark	Relative
BASIC INDUSTRIES	4.47	3.47	1
Chemicals	0.57	0.86	-0.3
Construct & Build Mats	3.89	2.42	1.46
Forestry & Paper	0	0.04	-0.04
Steel & Other Metals	0.01	0.14	-0.13
CYCLICAL CONSUMER GOODS	0.62	0.38	0.24
Automobiles & Parts	0.53	0.3	0.23
Household Goods & Text	0.09	0.08	0.01
CYCLICAL SERVICES	21.25	14.2	7.05
Distributors	0	0	0
General Retailers	1.89	3.11	-1.22
Leisure, Ent & Hotels	7.7	2.45	5.24
Media & Photography	5.94	4	1.95
Rest, Pubs & Breweries	0	0	0
Support Services	3.99	2.77	1.22
Transport	1.74	1.88	-0.14
FINANCIALS	26.78	27.63	-0.85
Banks	12.35	18	-5.65
Insurance	3.51	0.58	2.93
Investment Companies	0.48	2.6	-2.11
Life Assurance	0.94	2.93	-1.99
Real Estate	5.65	2	3.66
Speciality & Other Fin	3.84	1.52	2.32
GENERAL INDUSTRIALS	5.86	2.86	3
Aerospace & Defence	3.02	1.52	1.5
Diversified Industrial	0.06	0	0.06
Electronic & Electric	0.68	0.26	0.42
Engineering & Machine	2.1	1.08	1.02
INFORMATION TECHNOLOGY	3.36	0.99	2.37
Info Tech Hardware	1.15	0.28	0.87
Software & Comp Svcs	2.21	0.71	1.5
NON-CYCLICAL CONS GOODS	7.99	17.95	-9.96
Beverages	0.38	3.13	-2.75
Food Producers & Proc	1.2	2.45	-1.24
Health	0.47	0.47	0
Packaging	0	0	0
Personal Care & Hhold	0.02	0.92	-0.91
Pharmaceuticals & Bio	4.11	8.67	-4.56
Tobacco	1.81	2.3	-0.5
NON-CYCLICAL SERVICES	6.56	10.96	-4.39
Food & Drug Retailers	1.44	2.41	-0.96
Telecommunication Svcs	5.12	8.55	-3.43
RESOURCES	21.06	17.18	3.88
Mining	4.47	4.27	0.2
Oil & Gas	16.59	12.91	3.68
UTILITIES	2.05	4.38	-2.32
Electricity	1.97	1.57	0.4
Gas Distribution	0.05	1.76	-1.71
Water	0.03	1.04	-1.01

Source: BARRA

At this point, you might be forgiven for asking "how is BARRA related to past performance?" Isn't this the analysis of current information rather than the past? In fact that is not what the software does. In order to decide whether the portfolio is 'risky' or not, it looks instead at the past performance of the stocks that it sees in the portfolio. Each stock is categorized according to how its price has behaved over the past few years, e.g. its volatility, how far it has diverged from the index, and so on. As a result, each holding is categorised as being part of a sub-group, sector and so on. By looking at all the stocks together, the software can then give a view on the overall characteristics of the portfolio, but it is definitely using past performance to do so.

There are other proprietary systems too, some developed by professional fund investors. As it happens, my team has also developed our own software programme that does a similar job. We use monthly data in order to find how well a manager has fared relative to what you would expect him (or her) to do, given the 'style' of his fund, over a particular time period. I have given an example of a good (Invesco Perpetual Income) and a bad fund (Aegon UK Equity) below. You can see that the former has consistently added value (more bars above the line) whereas the latter has a much more mixed record.

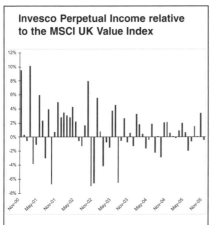

Source: Lipper, Total Return GBP to 30th Nov 2005

A short cut to style analysis

Given that the necessary software might be out of your price bracket, is there a method that a normal investor could use to try to see what drives a fund manager's performance? As long as you have access to the raw data, that is to say the price history of the fund you are interested in, although it is not infallible, there is a rough and ready means of checking on the style and risk characteristics of a fund. You can find a charting tool that will plot for you the performance of a fund on any number of websites, including www.trustnet.co.uk, www.morningstar.co.uk, www.fundsnetwork.co.uk, and so on. (The important thing is to go back far enough so as to be sure of capturing a full cycle of market experience. Ten years is a good time span to look at.)

To do a quick check on the likely style of a fund, what you need to do is focus in on periods when a particular style of investing was popular, and see how the fund you are interested in performed over that particular time frame. The best example in recent history was the period leading up to the peak of the internet bubble, namely the six months from September 1999 to March 2000. This was, par excellence, the period when 'growth stock investing' was at its most popular, and by contrast the period when 'value investing' was most out of favour.

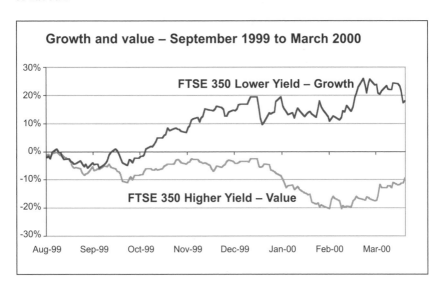

Source: Lipper/FTSE, Total Return in GBP

If you look at the performance of fund managers investing in the UK market over those six months, you will see in stark relief what sort of investors they were at the time. This in turn provides some clues as to what kind of investors they are likely to be now. Those that did very well are likely to be growth-orientated investors (although note that this is only the case when the same fund manager is in place and the fund itself is still pursuing the same investment objective: you have to be sure that you are comparing like with like for the conclusions to remain valid). Those that trailed are likely to have a 'value style'. You can see who appear to be the best at these contrasting disciplines as well.

Those that used the growth technique made a lot of money during those hectic six months, only to lose it all over the next three years, when the growth bubble burst in style. During this period, many 'value investors', such as the highly regarded Neil Woodford of Invesco Perpetual, lost money as the shares they had bought dropped – they were 'cheap' when he bought them and only became 'cheaper' still. Many 'value' funds fell by as much as 20%, but then made good money over the next three years as their style of investing came roaring back into favour.

The end result over those three years was that only eight fund managers made any money at all. The vast majority of the 271 funds in the two main equity market sectors, UK Income & UK All Companies, that were in operation over the whole period, lost money. In some cases the amounts involved were considerable. Could that have been avoided? In my view, the answer to that question goes to the heart of what successful fund investing is all about. And my answer is: yes, it could have been avoided and should not have resulted in such significant losses for investors.

Top and bottom performers – UK funds in 1999/2000 and 2000/2003

	31 Aug 1999 to 31 Mar 2000	31 Mar 2000 to 31 Mar 2003	31 Aug 1999 to 31 Mar 2003
Rathbone Income	1.28%	10.73%	12.14%
Fidelity Special Situations	7.41%	4.03%	11.74%
Credit Suisse Income	(-1.68%)	12.95%	11.05%
Solus UK Special Situations	119.77%	(-50.87%)	7.97%
Invesco Perpetual High Income	(-8.70%)	3.70%	(-5.33%)
Artemis Capital	76.97%	(-47.40%)	(-6.92%)
Norwich UK Growth	71.88%	(-53.51%)	(-20.09%)
FTSE All Share Index	7.12%	(-39.35%)	(-35.03%)
Manek Growth	93.55%	(-73.03%)	(-47.80%)

Source: Lipper, Total Return in GBP

Caveat emptor – a case study

Invesco European Growth was a fund that was all the rage in the mid and late 1990s. Run with a 'growth' bias, this fund was 2nd in its sector in 1993, 14th in 1994, 3rd in 1995, 2nd in 1996, had a poor 1997 being only 40th though still making its investors a healthy 25%, but leapt back to form in 1998 coming 1st, followed by a 2nd place in 1999. Any investor who had put money in at the start of 1993 had turned £1,000 into £7,133, a remarkable return, which was more than double that of the European sector average (which had only increased to £3,855).

Sadly as is often the way, many investors came rather late to the party, investing in late 1999 and early 2000. This was a pity, since in the event, the fund came one from bottom in 2000, absolutely bottom in 2001, and 74th (9th decile) in both 2002 and 2003. Someone who had invested at the end of 1999 on the basis of the preceding seven years performance would have seen every £1,000 they had invested fall to just £653 by the middle of 2005. This was a less than sparkling return, and well below that of the best performer, Fidelity European, which would have been worth £1,785, (closely followed in 3rd and 4th place by the two Jupiter funds in that sector!).

The lesson to draw from this saga is that good individuals do indeed add significant value for their investors, but it is important to understand what sort of investor they are, and therefore what conditions they will do well or badly in. The manager of the Invesco fund, as I have said, was a 'growth' investor, which served him well up until the technology bubble, when growth stocks were all the rage. The after-effects of that episode however meant that many of the stocks he was invested in did particularly badly after March 2000, and in the nature of things, many investors chose to invest their money during the bubble period – when the fund's performance track record was at its best. The upshot was that the manager of the fund bought much larger chunks of his favoured companies at what turned out to be very wrong prices.

Look out for hockey sticks

It is worth pointing out that if you ever see a chart of a fund's performance that looks like a 'hockey stick', as the one below does, beware. Such a formation is often a warning of a setback ahead. The charts shown here are those of the Invesco Perpetual European Growth fund, described above, and Fidelity European. When logarithmic (see Glossary) charts go into hockey stick shape, it usually means that the performance of a fund is accelerating at an unsustainable rate. You don't want to be buying a fund at that point, though it will be the very moment that its past performance looks at its best. The common sense observation on this is again, that when something seems too good to be true, it usually is!

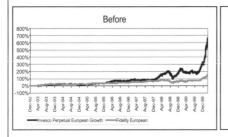

Before

Source: Lipper, Total return in GBP to 10.03.2000, relative to the IMA Europe ex UK Sector average

After

Source: Lipper, Total return in GBP to 30.09.2005, relative to the IMA Europe ex UK Sector average

Much has been written about the dotcom 'bubble', which is how the last six months of the long bull market in shares have come to be known. The sadness about it is that so many ordinary investors lost money they may need for their retirement. However, bubbles have come and gone for hundreds of years, and there will be more. They are often not recognised as such whilst they are happening, which is why they affect so many people. But if you follow the 'hockey stick' principle, you will not go far wrong (see above).

However, there are always a few people who do recognise what is going on. There are clues that, as a smart investor, you try to pick up. As an example, I remember seeing a very small advertisement in a Sunday newspaper for a property fund in February 2000, at the height of the bubble, issued by Richard Timberlake's then company Portfolio Fund Management. It caught the eye because, despite its small size, it was so different to everything else that was being touted around at the time.

Richard Timberlake is one of the innovators in the UK fund management industry and someone whose knowledge and intuition I greatly respect. The fact he thought property was a good bet at a time when the asset class was so out of favour with marketing people, was a factor in persuading me and my colleagues that the bull market was nearly over. We fortunately changed the stance of our funds in March 2000, thereby ensuring that our performance did not suffer as badly as that of many other funds.

In summary, the important thing in ensuring that you aren't hurt by the next bubble is to make sure that all your investments are based on sound financial principles. Keep your feet on the ground.

The dangers in past performance

To return to the mirror analogy, over the years I have used the example of the Brighton Hall of Mirrors when discussing these quantitative techniques that look at portfolios and performance. As I said earlier, when you look in a mirror you see a reflection of yourself. What you see in the Hall of Mirrors is the same thing, manipulated by each mirror. Some make you look tall and thin, others short and fat, others wavy and so on. The same is true of all the various types of statistics and ratios that come out of the software programmes I have mentioned. They are all, in the last resort, based on the same historic data – and assume that what happened in the recent past will continue into the future.

All the software programmes are sophisticated and, when sold commercially, expensive. Each system has its pluses and minuses. There is no doubt that they do provide some useful additional information for determining how a fund manager goes about his business. A fund manager who says he is a value investor, for example, but in practice spends most of his time investing in growth stocks is almost certainly not one you want to have your money with. Either the manager does not realise what is happening (which is an obvious negative) or he does know, yet for some reason wishes to conceal the fact from the investors in the fund (which is an equally obvious negative).

But at the same time, there is no amount of statistical analysis that will tell you for sure how a fund will perform in the future. There are two reasons for this. One is that the market itself moves in mysterious ways, particularly in the short-term. If you cannot find out where the market is going to go tomorrow, it follows that you cannot tell which style is going to be dominant either (although you might be able to make an educated guess). The second reason is that there are other circumstances, such as a change of fund manager, which could mean that a particular fund will not behave in the same way as it has done in the past.

You have to use all these things with great care. Software programmes can analyse the past very precisely. You can judge, for example, how effective a particular fund manager was at a certain stage in the past, say, during the run-up to the start of the first Gulf War in 1990. But you have to allow for the fact that while some people learn by experience, others who are in the 'right place at the right time' can fail to take on board the appropriate conclusions from whatever happened to their portfolio. As a result, they might not perform as well as analysis of the historic numbers might lead you to suppose that they would.

Other interpretation problems

To summarise therefore, using past performance can be a way to investigate whether a fund manager possesses real skill. Arriving at a verdict is not simple, however. It requires a reasonably sophisticated knowledge and understanding of investments, a considerable database of price performance, and knowledge of the industry. Interestingly, trawling the numbers over a long period of time shows that bad performance has a greater likelihood of being repeated in the future than good performance.

There are a number of other potential problems. Firstly, there is a major one for those of you who are reading this book to try and determine whether your segregated portfolio manager (whether he is managing an individual account, a charity or a firm's pension fund) is any good. The performance record of your fund is unlikely to be available in sufficient enough detail to draw any conclusions. Secondly, many investors may not be aware which individual manages their fund, and for how long they have been at their post. It can be discovered reasonably easily, but does require effort on your part.

Research conducted by my team's competitors at Credit Suisse shows the average tenure of a fund manager on a fund is roughly three years. Research into the performance record, therefore, may not have any relevance at all. Thirdly, but more rarely, there can be managers who create good performance by doing one thing, without actually saying as such to the outside world, then going on to manage money in a completely different manner. So, research into their track record may be genuinely misleading.

Not all he appeared to be

One fund manager I know made their name during the dotcom boom with staggeringly good performance. This manager was described in the marketing literature as being a 'value investor'. A couple of years later, it was confirmed to me that the amazing performance of the fund during those heady times had not in fact come from ordinary value investing – very much the opposite. Traditionally value investors are meant to be patient, ready to wait months or years for their favoured shares to come back into favour. Not so this one. "We used to flip (sell straight away) new issues like they were going out of fashion," I was told. "If we didn't think they would go to at least a 20% premium, we didn't bother with them. They weren't worth the effort."

It may not have been fundamental investment as most people would define it, but it certainly made his investors a lot of money. Unlike many, this manager was sensible enough to realise what was going on and that the crazy market conditions of 1999-2000 could not persist. From February 2000 onwards he used the money that new investors had put in his fund to buy genuine value stocks, such as tobacco companies, which had been hammered during the bubble, but which then started rising inexorably. The moral is that you do need to look behind the figures. Analysis of the past performance of his fund might lead someone who didn't know the facts to draw misleading conclusions.

Enter the regulators

Because of the dangers in using past performance as a guide to which funds to buy, all Jupiter's advertisements carry the warning: "Past performance is no guide to future returns and the value of investments can fall as well as rise." Every single piece of advertising and marketing literature approved by UK authorised and regulated financial services firms must now carry this piece of rubric. (I rather like the way that the iconoclastic firm Bedlam Asset Management dealt with this requirement in 2002, after two years of falling share prices. Its advertisements declared: "The value of an investment and the income from it can go up as well as down", thus complying, even if tongue in cheek, with the UK Financial Services Authority requirements).

One result of the FSA's insistence on warnings about past performance is that almost everyone these days seems to assume that this is an empirical fact. In this approach they are encouraged by the marketing efforts of the large index-tracking firms, and given comfort by lazy parts of the media who keep running with the story. I hope that this chapter has shown that you can draw conclusions from what has happened to funds and fund managers in the past, and by extension about what might happen in the future. But you have to proceed with care.

Points to remember

1. Picking funds solely on the basis of past performance is unlikely to be profitable.
2. That does not mean that there is nothing of value to be gained from studying the way funds have performed in the past.
3. Analysing when and in what conditions particular funds do well can help you to identify the managers who have demonstrated real skill.
4. Managers of funds don't always do what they say they are doing. Many move jobs frequently.
5. Taking care when interpreting past performance data is essential, as the regulators say.

7

The truth about costs (and index funds)

"Men occasionally stumble over the truth, but most of them pick themselves up and hurry off as if nothing ever happened."

Sir Winston Churchill

Do costs matter that much?

If you read a lot of newspaper or academic comment, you will find that plenty has been written about the high costs of investing in funds. Much has also been written about the 'shocking' fact that too many funds underperform the markets as represented by the FTSE All Share Index. It would be easy for the casual observer to think from reading this kind of comment that investing in funds was a waste of time.

I like to see the mediocre challenged, but my problem with studies claiming to show that picking the best funds is virtually impossible to do, and that costs are all that matter, is that it flies in the face of common sense. Surely it is likely that there are some professional investors out there who can 'beat the market'? Otherwise how can it be that there are plenty of investors who lose money to the market consistently? Somebody has to be profiting at their expense, and costs alone cannot be the explanation.

In fact, the unit trust industry is unusual in that it is very easy for customers to see what the costs are of using its products. The same cannot be said of the life insurance industry, where the costs to the investor are much more opaque (and generally higher). Yet the combined total of life assurance products managed by life companies is around £900bn whereas that managed by the unit trust and OEIC industry is valued at nearer £300bn. Why is this so? There are a number of structural reasons, but I think that one of the main ones is people tend to be less price-sensitive when that price is hidden from them, or is made so difficult to understand that the effort of working it out is too much for them.

Too little competition on price

As many commentators have noted, there doesn't seem to be much price competition in the world of savings and investment. But there is considerable competition in terms of brand, brand values, performance and service. The main reason for the lack of price competition must be that there is a great deal of inertia amongst investors. Poor performance is tolerated for long periods of time by investors. This in turn gives fund groups little incentive to change.

For instance, the Invesco Perpetual European Growth fund, whose performance was highlighted in the last chapter, still has nearly £1bn invested in it, despite its terrible recent track record. It has been the second worst performer in the European sector over the last five and a half years, losing you 30% more than the sector average! That is quite astounding! Yet it is still the 44th biggest fund out of the 1,857 unit trusts and OEICs currently in existence. The implication is that investors either haven't noticed what a poor return they have had, or simply do not wish to know.

In this instance, it is true that there are some mitigating factors. Early investors made significant gains and may not have wished to sell because of their capital gains tax position – if they sold the fund, they would have to pay tax on their gains. Secondly, the manager of the fund was changed in July 2003, and since then the fund has performed in line with the sector average and beaten the FTSE European Index. While the performance has not been exceptional, many investors may reckon that it is, at least, now acceptable.

If investors are slow to take money out of funds that have done poorly, the choice facing the fund management group is either to make changes to improve the performance (and so attract new investors) or to 'closet index' the fund. By so doing they can try and retain as much of the funds' assets as they can. Closet indexing is the way of managing a fund so that, in practice, it resembles an index fund, while purporting to be something rather more dynamic. As performance sells units, a change in fund manager is often the first response you will see to a poorly performing fund. But what they are unlikely to do is cut their fees as they can assume clients are so apathetic that they aren't going to desert the fund anyway. This applies all the way across the industry.

My conclusion, underlined by the amount of money that continues to languish in large numbers of underperforming funds, must be that investors tolerate mediocrity or worse for too long. In fact they are agonisingly slow to move their money. The irony is that fund advertisements, at the FSA's requirement, tell you that investments in equity funds should only be considered for a minimum of five years. That is fair enough if you have a good fund manager running your money; to change funds too frequently will add unnecessary transaction charges. But is this really such good advice if you are in a 'no hope fund'? I think not. However, hope springs eternal and the lethargy of many investors is astonishing.

A more logical state of affairs

In my view, as I have said, it is people who make the difference in fund management, and it is the smartest and most reliable people who are more likely to produce good performance. Logically it would be sensible to expect the better people to charge a higher price for their services. In terms of the price of funds it is not generally true for funds run by mainstream institutions, where the standard annual management fee of 1.5% tends to apply. However, I predict that with the gradual adoption of the new fund regulations (known as 'COLL') (see Glossary), which will be mandatory by February 2007, the price of funds run by the small number of exceptional investors will go up. This has already been seen in the higher fees of funds run by excellent managers at many boutique investment firms.

Is that such a bad thing? If you are lucky enough to have come across the next Anthony Bolton, Fidelity's star fund manager, or Philip Gibbs, one of my colleagues at Jupiter, it has to make sense to be prepared to pay a higher price for their services than for mediocrity. The only issue is whether the additional cost is likely to eliminate entirely the extra performance that they are capable of achieving. Simple maths tells you that a fund that costs you 2% per annum more will have to outperform by at least that amount if it is to justify charging more than the average. It can be done. Bolton's Fidelity Special Situations fund has beaten the FTSE All Share Index by an average of 6% per annum over 25 years, while charging, for most of that period, the same standard 1.5% annual management charge as his less successful competitors.

As the relative outperformance of the best fund managers tends to diminish the larger their funds become, it will hardly be a surprise if their employers seek to charge investors who want to have money managed by the best, a higher fee. (If fund managers could repeat their performance regardless of fund size, the management company could continue to grow its profits merely by taking as much money as possible into the fund.) Nonetheless, I hope that we are not about to witness the start of a general upward trend in the cost of all funds regardless of quality. That would not be to the benefit of investors.

The fund of funds example

My own particular area of expertise is multi-manager funds. The idea behind multi-manager funds is a simple but powerful one, at least if you agree with my view that a small number of fund managers who can make a difference do exist and that it is possible to identify them. If you cannot find the best fund managers yourself, why not hire a professional to do the job for you? That is what I and my colleagues in Jupiter's fund of funds team spend our time doing. We use our professional resources and experience to put together portfolios of 15-20 of the very best funds, which we then manage for investors in the normal way.

The story is good, but I have to say that the way this idea works out in practice is not always quite so appealing. The vast majority of multi-managers, in my view, pay too much attention to the issue of price, and too little to the issue of quality. While they say that their aim is to invest with the best, they all too often fail to practise what they preach. As a result, in many fund of funds operations, the investor ends up with a shapeless fund that is far too large.

If you add up the individual shareholdings owned by the various underlying funds in many fund of funds portfolios, some of them own as many as 4,000 or more underlying shares. They are effectively diversifying away most of their potential for outperformance. Such funds are often managed very tightly against their benchmarks, meaning that they are not expected to deviate very far from the performance of the index. This further reduces their performance potential. Taken together with the extra layer of fees involved, this means that they have very little chance of producing above average returns for investors.

Not all funds of funds are like that, but as with any other financial product you need to understand what you are buying. The general point is that when selecting funds, cheaper is not necessarily better. Of course if you have two identical products, and one is cheaper than the other, it makes sense to buy the one that costs you less. But you must recognise the assumption that has been made here, which is that we are discussing two identical products. While that may be true of index funds, it is not necessarily the case with actively managed funds. Indeed, the whole point of actively managed funds is to produce something different from the average, so it is illogical to expect them to cost the same.

When you look at the annual costs of a fund, it is very easy to see the potential effect of costs over a number of years. For instance, say a fund has an annual cost of 1.5% and its investments grow in value at a steady rate of 10% per annum for 20 years. You can calculate that before costs, such an investment would increase from £10,000 to £61,159. But after the application of a 1.5% per annum management charge the investment will only have risen to £45,893, a difference of £15,266, or 25% (see the chart below). It follows that if you are paying a 1.5% fee per annum for a fund, you need to be confident that the manager is capable of beating the market by a similar margin. Otherwise you will be no better off than if you had picked a fund that was cheaper and had no performance advantage. An index fund falls into that category, or would do if it had no charges at all. (In practice, of course, they do.)

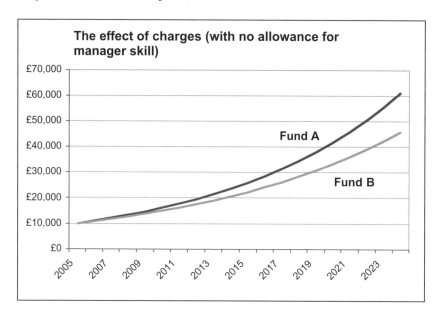

Source: John Chatfeild-Roberts

An imperfect market?

What is the right price for a fund? The answer must be what the market will bear. Unfortunately, economic theory assumes that all participants have equal access to the same information, and that their knowledge is, therefore, 'perfect'. It is the case, however, that investors are not all equally informed. Moreover, although there are many well informed investors, there are also a large number who have not even been taught or learnt any of the principles of investment and so are at the mercy of events. It must make sense for a government, of whatever hue, to make it a priority to teach children basic financial literacy in schools. It could be combined within the mathematics curriculum and also later on in general studies. People should be responsible for their own futures and I think that society would be better for a higher level of financial debate.

What about index funds?

Low costs form the basis for one half of the argument for investing in index-tracking funds. They are usually cheaper than actively managed funds and so the inhibiting effect of the annual management charge is minimised. It has to be said though, that there are plenty of index funds out there that have annual fees of 1%, which in the context of what we are discussing is hardly cheap. However that pales in comparison to the very expensive Legal and General Stockmarket Trust (a FTSE 100 tracker) which has an annual management fee of a staggering 2%!

If you had invested £10,000 in this fund at launch on the 28th May 1993 your investment at the end of August 2005 would have been worth £21,660. In other words, a return of 116.6%. You might think you had done quite well. Sad to say, however, this is not the case. The FTSE 100 Index itself returned 180.8% with dividends reinvested, and even the IMA UK All Companies sector average generated 179.8%. In other words, the index itself turned £10,000 into £28,060, and the index tracker underperformed the index it was meant to be 'tracking' by a massive 63.2% over those twelve years. If you do the calculation, over its twelve or so years the fund has underperformed the index by roughly 2.6% every year. That is even more than the hefty 2% annual management fee.

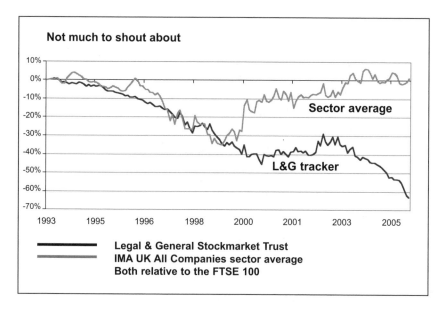

Not much to shout about

Source: Lipper, percentage growth total return, tax default in GBP to 30th September 2005

Now one example does not prove a theory, but it is fair to say that a passive index-tracking fund is almost guaranteed to do one thing and that is to underperform the index that it is trying to track by roughly the amount of its annual charges, despite attempts to mitigate the effect through such things as income from stock-lending. Personally, I have not found any examples in the UK retail marketplace to disprove this in my research over the years (see Appendix 2). So in the case of an index-tracker, unlike actively managed funds, and assuming that it is efficiently managed, it is true to say that cheaper will be better.

Footnote: To be fair to the company concerned, this fund has only around £40m invested in it, whereas the rather larger L&G UK Index Trust (£3.2bn), which tracks the FTSE All Share Index, has a better history as a result of its lower costs, although it also underperforms its index.

The trouble with indices

Apart from costs, there are other problems with index tracking. The technology bubble was certainly an extraordinary event, and as well as the individual financial dislocation that it caused, it also exposed the fact that there are weaknesses in the make-up of many indices. There have been arguments over the years as to whether you should have arithmetic or geometric indices, whether all companies represented in them should have equal weightings, whether the index should only use the 'free float' i.e. be a completely investable index, and so on. You can easily find adherents on all sides. There are many vested interests with money at stake, and examples of many different varieties of index across the world.

What happened in 2000 was that many of the major stock market indices, such as the FTSE 100 in the UK, became completely distorted by the relentless rise of the 'dotcoms'. Because it was a 'bubble', in which investors lost sight of reality, by definition very few people recognised it as such. Even the *Financial Times* had a proud banner on the back of its first section at the time, declaring it to be 'The Newspaper of the New Economy'. (This is a good example of the cheerleaders in a bubble, pointed out by Dr Sandy Nairn in his book on technology bubbles 'Engines That Move Markets', published by John Wiley & Sons Inc 2002.) The indices reflected the distortions of the bubble, to the detriment of many investors. Real companies with real sales, profits and assets were unceremoniously ejected from indices as the ever increasing value of 'ethereal companies' meant that, according to the rules, they had to be promoted into these indices.

There are many extraordinary examples, with the top of this crazy market episode being marked by the flotation of Lastminute.com. The rise of the dotcoms is fascinating in itself as a manifestation of a mania, but it was a nightmare for the tracker funds, which had to scramble to buy these stocks at any price and at considerable cost to their investors. You may say that we are no longer in bubble territory, but the problem for trackers still exists. As a result of a capital reorganisation, for example, Shell now makes up roughly double the amount of the FTSE 100 Index that it did in 2004. Index trackers had to buy the shares, irrespective of their attractiveness. Whenever you have investors who are not allowed to use their brains, anomalies are bound to occur, and money will inevitably be lost.

Active managers can win

The second half of the argument in favour of passive investment is that no actively managed fund ever beats the index consistently, so you might as well invest in the index instead. The previous chapter has addressed this issue. However to recap, it can be seen that there are talented individuals out there, many of whom I have met over the years, who do have the ability to add value by beating the market over a long period of time. If you do not feel you are likely to be able to identify and invest with them, that is your prerogative – but don't be fooled into thinking that it cannot be done.

Looking at the data, it has always been my suspicion that the numbers used to prove the superiority of tracker funds tend to be selectively chosen. However, I am sure some of you may expect me to produce some of my own to justify my common sense assertions. Reliable and honest data is hard to find further back than the mid 1980s although indices have existed for far longer. The particular problem is that data including reinvested dividends, without the use of which any figures must be suspect, is not widely available before the start of 1986. So I have run crude performance data since the FTSE All Share Index was available on a dividend reinvested basis, which is from the 31st December 1985, i.e. the last 20 years. I have combined the IMA UK All Companies and UK Income Sectors, which essentially cover the majority of funds available to an investor wanting to invest in the UK stock market. The following points are notable:

- All the 96 funds (bar one) beat cash, as measured by the Bank of England Base Rate, over 20 years; and 178 out of 189 beat cash over ten years.

- 37 funds, or 39% of the total, beat the Index over 20 years.

- Of those that beat the Index over the first ten years, 72% of them (i.e. 27) repeated the feat, beating the Index over the subsequent ten years.

- Of those (59 funds) that lagged the Index over the first ten years, 68% again failed beat it over the next ten years.

- UK Equity Income funds, with dividends reinvested, performed considerably better as a group than UK All Companies funds.

- There were no index trackers in the sample as none had been launched in 1985.

This data looks solely at funds rather than fund managers, which in itself is a flaw in my view. The figures demonstrate that good performance is repeatable, but also underline the fact that you need only be concerned with a minority of funds. Of course it is not feasible for all investors to beat the market, and fewer of them can do so consistently. But it is a considerable intellectual leap from saying that you personally cannot identify those people to saying that it is not possible for anyone to do so. The point is that, while it may be hard work, the rewards of finding the best people can be considerable. Out of over 4,000 possible funds available in the UK, you only need to find 10-15 good ones to have a powerful portfolio. That is less than 1% of the total.

You still have to make decisions

The final problem with a passive investment strategy is that anyone who would prefer not to make any decisions at all about their investments (which is one of the main reasons advanced for choosing an index fund) will quickly find that they don't have the luxury of that option. For starters, which index would you like to track? The index industry has been growing very fast over the last fifteen years, largely as a result of the fashion for passive investing, and the parallel growth in derivatives (see Glossary). But you may be surprised to know that Lipper lists over 13,000 indices on the database that we use, of which over 3,200 come from FTSE alone.

The choice of what you choose to track is hardly simple. Truly passive investment doesn't exist, in the sense that there is no one index that perfectly captures the full spectrum of potential investment markets. Instead there is a broad range of indices, covering a wide variety of markets, each with slightly different characteristics. As a fund investor, merely by picking one index rather than another you are, in effect, being forced to take a view. It may or may not be a good view, but it will have consequences for the returns you make, and the risks you take.

Conclusion

There is now over £12bn invested in UK index-tracking unit trusts. It would be foolish to say that this does not say something about the performance of some actively managed funds as a group, and/or the naïveté of those who invest in them. The answer for those who have had bad experiences with actively managed funds, and are tempted by index funds is not to put all your faith in passive management. Instead try rather harder to make better fund choices.

All the money that is tied up in index funds will not, I believe, be good news for those who own those assets (many of which are in pension funds). But it is certainly great news for active investors. The more money that becomes passively managed, the more potential profits there are to be made by the best active investors at their expense. As the recent recipient of an investment award said on receiving his prize: "I would just like to say thank you to all those index trackers out there who have created the opportunities to be exploited!"

Points to remember

1. Costs are an important factor when deciding which funds to buy, but should not dominate your thinking.

2. The costs of funds are more visible than those of many other investment products, including life company products.

3. The chances are that the cost of the best funds will start to rise in future years.

4. Many funds of funds focus on cost at the expense of quality and are too broadly diversified to add real value.

5. Index funds are not a panacea for all investment ills – taking more care in picking actively managed funds is a better option for investors willing to make the effort.

Asset allocation and managing risk

"Risk comes from not knowing what you are doing."
Warren Buffett

"When I look back on all these worries, I remember the story of the old man who said on his deathbed that he had had a lot of trouble in his life, most of which had never happened."

Sir Winston Churchill

What does asset allocation really mean?

Different people mean different things by asset allocation, the jargon the fund industry uses to describe how to split your money between different areas. Some believe it describes the moving of money from one part of the globe to another. But I prefer to think of it as looking at the bigger picture, trying to spot the developing multi-year trends, and then investing accordingly. That said, it is clear that investment needs to be considered in a global rather than in a narrow regional or national context. Companies operate globally and so should investors. The range of funds open to investors makes global investing an easy reality today.

In fact, investments can be categorised in a variety of different ways; by country, by industry/sector and by style, to name three subdivisions. In practice, none of these is mutually exclusive. For instance, you could have a Hong Kong listed company that operates in the manufacturing sector and is classified as a 'growth company'. But this does not mean, for example, that all Hong Kong companies are defined as 'growth companies', and it is obvious that they are not all in the manufacturing sector.

There are potential opportunities at each level. Sometimes it makes sense to move money to a particular country, perhaps where the economy is recovering. At other times, it may be right to increase your exposure to a particular sector, such as financials or resources. There are times to be in growth shares and times, such as the last few years, to be in value shares instead. Anyone who operates in my field has to be ready to form a view about the best balance of assets to own in these various categories.

What do professional investors do? The majority tend to invest their clients' money according to a set of received orthodoxies. The most commonly used parameter is geographical asset allocation. In the 1980s and 1990s the managers of most UK pension funds looked closely at their geographical weightings. Many still do. For them, where their investments were based was a more important factor than which industry those investments were in. However, as you can imagine, investments do not always move neatly in line with the regions in which they are situated. For instance, during 2005, the fact that a share had been in the resources sector would have been far more important for its performance than whether it was listed in London or New York.

> **Weightings**
>
> *Geographical weightings, in a fund management context, are the percentage amounts of a fund that are invested in different countries. In today's global economy, the results can sometimes be misleading. A company such as BP, while its shares are listed in London, derives most of its earnings from outside the UK.*

Others eschew the geographical approach and say that because information is so freely available globally, it only makes sense to invest on a sector by sector basis. That might mean comparing cement companies around the world, and investing in those which either have the best growth prospects or are the cheapest. This is estimable as an approach. A lot of money has been made through spotting such global anomalies in recent years. Unfortunately, it has also led some investors to the position where they feel they have to have exposure to all the available sectors in the market, regardless of their merits. Some sectors, such as technology, would have been best avoided in the last five years.

Don't be too rigid

In my view, it is far more important for investors to choose investments that go up, rather than stick rigidly to a particular asset allocation formula. There really is no point in having investments in funds that you think will go down in price just because your 'process' says that you have to have so much of your clients' money invested in that type of fund. All the approaches mentioned have their merits. I believe that the key, as an investor, or as a professional, is to form a view about where the best opportunities lie, and make your investments accordingly. Having said that, it is fair to say that asset allocation is a subject which provokes heated debate amongst investment professionals.

On the one hand, many say that it is virtually impossible to add value through asset allocation and therefore that it is not worth trying to do so. This is an argument that is reminiscent of that deployed by the index-tracking fraternity, and suffers from the same defect. Just because many people find it difficult to do a job effectively does not mean that the job is not worth doing at all. That is an obvious fallacy. Others say that it is a high risk activity and that they do not believe their clients should be exposed to the risks of asset allocation going wrong – proof, as if it were needed, that there are plenty of defeatist investors out there!

I take the rather more pragmatic view that the duty of any investment professional is to try to make money for his clients, not to bleat about how difficult something is. It follows that you must be prepared to try and take advantage of every reasonable opportunity to make money. In other words, you should be prepared to use all the 'tools in the toolbox'. That includes taking asset allocation decisions where you sincerely believe, having studied the available evidence, that you can add something of value to the investor's portfolio and wealth.

In the case of funds, that means not only choosing the best fund managers you can find in each area, but looking for the ones who have 'the wind behind them', in the sense of operating in the sectors or countries you think will do best. Many people say, however, that such an active approach will mean that your portfolio has to be subjected to high turnover, as you move it to react to every twist and turn of the investment breeze.

This, they point out, is an inherently bad practice – to which I reply "it all depends". High turnover for its own sake is to be avoided at any cost, but it is wrong to be too dogmatic about when and how often you make changes in your overall asset allocation.

The first point to bring out is that if you make a correct decision, the costs of that change pale into insignificance compared to the opportunity cost of not making it. Remember that you often have to be quick to take advantage of an opportunity before the 'market' has spotted it and the opportunity has gone.

The second is that in reality asset allocation is more often about long-term choices, not short-term tactical trading. It involves blocking out the 'noise' of every day's newspapers and looking at the bigger picture. Common sense plays its part here, together with good information and investment analysis. What are the really big themes in the world and who is making money out of them? What is everyone talking about, and probably more importantly, what are most people ignoring?

Keep yourself informed

Plenty of **good** reading is the key here – and in these days of the internet, it doesn't take that much effort to track down, even if it may not be free. Good examples of lateral thinking sites are: www.Independent-Investor.com, www.BreakingViews.com, www.FinTrend.com, www.Smithers.co.uk, www.GloomBoomDoom.com, www.SmartMoney.com, www.PrudentBear.com, www.HaysMarketFocus.com. There are plenty of others, but the key is to make sure you don't just read one side of the argument.

There are always two sides to anything, and part of the art of asset allocation is to work out when a view is right; some people have the same view all the time – we usually call them 'perma-bulls' or 'perma-bears'. For instance, as might be imagined, the Prudent Bear website tends to be on the side of the pessimists. The analogy of a stopped clock is useful here; it will be right twice a day but you don't know when, whereas a clock that loses a minute a day is always wrong, but not by very much! Useful information also may not come from the most obvious sources either, so the ability to think laterally is one to be cultivated.

The trouble with weightings

Returning to the practices of the investment industry, I am not sure that the arbitrary limits that fund managers place on themselves, or that are placed there by consultants, are really in the best interests of investors. Fund managers are often not allowed to let their holdings stray more than a certain amount away from the weighting that a country or a sector has in a particular index. For example, if banks account for, say, 15% of a particular country's stock market by capitalisation, a manager may be told that his portfolio must operate within 5% of that figure. In other words, his fund must own no less than 10%, and no more than 20%, in bank shares.

These limits are typically imposed in the name of risk control, but it seems to me to be more of an admission that nobody has much confidence in the capacity of the fund manager. Unfortunately the habit is now rife in the investment industry. It is one thing to limit your risk by diversifying; and another to deny yourself the chance to back your judgement when you (or your chosen fund manager) have confidence in a particular market or sector view.

Japan: a cautionary tale

At the end of 1989, Japan's stock market made up half of the world index by market capitalisation. Anyone who had an investment which closely resembled that index would have spent the next ten years becoming rather disenchanted with life. If you compare the performance of Japan to the performance of the US as in this chart you will see that there was a 400% difference! How can one then say that long-term asset allocation isn't worth the effort?

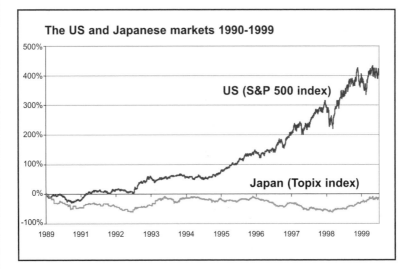

The US and Japanese markets 1990-1999

Source: Lipper, percentage growth total return, tax default in GBP to 31st December 1999

Another idea that makes me cynical, and which is similar in conception to shadowing an index, is that of fund managers investing their portfolios based on the average of what everyone else in their particular sector is doing. This is something that long held sway in pension fund investing (creating problems for many pension funds as a result). It still has many practitioners in both the institutional and retail worlds.

Let us think about this logically for a moment. To take a simple example, say there are three funds, A, B & C. Fund A has 15% of its money invested in UK shares whilst Fund B has 85% of its assets invested similarly. The manager of Fund C has meanwhile decided to benchmark himself against the average of what everyone else is doing. As the 'benchmark' has 50% in UK equities (15+85 divided by 2) and he doesn't want to take any 'risks', he also invests 50% of his fund in the UK. Where is the sense in that? Of course the reality is that, if there are a large number of funds in a particular universe, many of them trying to be close to the average performer, the result is bound to be that they do all end up very close to such an average. This in truth helps to explain why many large funds move so closely together, as the chart below shows.

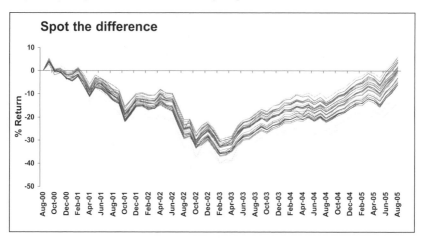

Performance of 'balanced managed' life funds over 1bn in size 2000-2005. There are some differences between the performance of large balanced funds run by life insurance companies, but in general their performance is much of a muchness and little different from average.

Source: Standard & Poor's total return in GBP to 31st August 2005

Whose risk is it anyway?

As before, this benchmarking is done in the name of risk reduction, but my question is whose risk is it that is being reduced? Most investors would argue that the idea of investment is to make their money grow over time. However there can be no guarantee that either an index, or the average of what everybody else is doing, is going to go up. In fact, when the market falls, the average fund is bound to do the same. So what we are talking about is purely relative, not absolute risk, reduction.

The risk that fund managers end up being concerned with, is whether they do worse than either the index or another fund manager working for a different firm, not whether they make money for their investors. The less leeway a fund manager is given, the less likely it is that his or her fund will deviate from the index or the average. In other words, it is the firm's business risk, or the fund manager's career risk, rather than the client's risk that is being targeted. People don't often get fired for doing what everyone else is doing, or for underperforming by relatively small amounts.

Either way, intuitively it doesn't seem a very sensible way to run someone's money for them. My advice, when looking for funds and fund managers is, if you are confident that you can find the good ones, use those who are not very concerned about 'benchmark risk'. Unless of course you yourself are worried by it.

Are absolute returns the answer?

We discussed the risk of total loss in Chapter Two. I think it is certainly true to say that for most private investors, the risk of losing money is a much more important risk than to lose money against a particular benchmark. There is academic theory to back this up. Professor Daniel Kahneman shared the Nobel Economics prize in 2002 for work that included observations on loss aversion. He found that we hate losing money far more than we like making it, which is why absolute return funds (particularly hedge funds) have become so popular after the ravages of a bear market.

Many of them are run by very clever people, and my team at Jupiter runs a successful fund of long/short equity funds, linking in with just such people. Unfortunately, rather like generals who fight the last war, people often buy what would have done them well last time round rather than what will be the best investment going forward. It is fair to say that we have had a bull market in shares since March 2003, yet only now are investors becoming more interested in equity funds and the rush into the hedge arena is slowing down.

> ### *Absolute and relative returns*
>
> *In the fund industry, funds fall into one of two categories. Absolute return funds have an objective to make positive returns in all periods, whereas relative return funds are set up to keep within a given distance of their benchmark index. So if the FTSE All Share Index falls 15% in a year, a relative return fund that only falls 10% will consider it has had a good year. For an absolute return fund, a 10% loss would be a very poor result.*

How not to allocate your assets

I came across a charity recently that had made a bit of a muddle with its equity exposure. It held equities, property and some fixed interest; but during the years 2000-2003 it didn't really have enough in fixed interest to protect its portfolio, although it had a higher than average exposure to property. After two and a half years of a bear market the trustees had had enough. They appointed investment consultants to advise them on their next move. The consultants opined that the charity should be concentrating on absolute returns, and that as a result their equity exposure was too high. You can guess the rest. April 2003 saw the start of the turn around in equity prices in the UK, and this opportunity of the slightest uptick in prices was seized to sell much of the equity exposure and convert it into fixed interest and hedge fund type holdings. As you can see from the chart, there has been a big difference in the performance of the UK equity market and the gilt market since then. And even hedge funds have by no means kept up, as indicated by the performance of the CSFB Tremont Hedge Fund Index which is nearly 30% behind the FTSE All Share Index. As all investment professionals should know, the timing of investments is absolutely crucial. The decision to go for absolute returns was by no means the wrong one over the longer term, but the timing of so doing for this particular charity was unfortunate in the extreme. In fact it was such bad timing that they will probably find it impossible ever to catch back up to where they would have been.

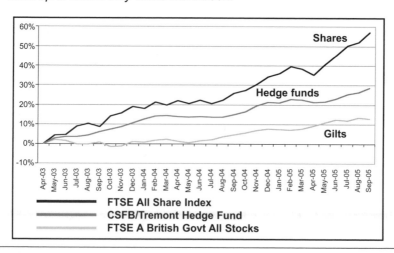

FTSE All Share Index
CSFB/Tremont Hedge Fund
FTSE A British Govt All Stocks

Source: Lipper, percentage growth total return, tax default, in local currency

Living with volatility

Chapter Two demonstrated that the risk of complete loss if you own a unit trust or OEIC is very low indeed. However as the risk warnings say, "Investments may rise and fall"; funds based on ordinary shares, rather than most (but not all) fixed interest stocks, do exhibit equity-like volatility and many people think that volatility is risk. The ups and downs of fund prices only matter to an investor, however, if they are planning to do something with that particular fund, and very often falls are more to do with general market sentiment than anything else. If you are a contrarian and want to take advantage of an opportunity, a fall in prices is a chance to add more money to the investment.

It is more common, however, to find the instinctive human reaction of increased pessimism when the price of a fund falls. If the investment is sound but you have no more money to invest, it is a better idea to ignore the drop in price or concentrate on the flow of dividends if it is income producing. You may wish to take the opportunity to revisit the investment, to make sure the fundamentals are still sound and that the manager is still in place.

In that regard, it can be useful to look at the investments underlying your fund, which are available in the six monthly fund reports, and increasingly commonly posted on investment companies' websites. It is worth looking at the valuation measures, such as yield or P/E ratio (see Glossary), of some of these underlying holdings (the ratios are available in newspapers). This will give you an indication of the way the fund is positioned and you can make a judgement as to whether that seems sensible to you.

But unless you think that you have found a better investment that will go up more than the one you have already, you should not sell up and sit in cash, as so many have done over the years. Crystallising a loss for no reason other than the price has fallen, and not re-investing the money, is a guaranteed way to produce substandard returns.

Generating above average returns for our clients is what I and my team are striving to do in our Jupiter Merlin funds of funds. We use the principles and ideas that I have written about so far; as our advertisements have said: "It is not rocket science", but there is nothing like an example to explain how we actually go about keeping a portfolio of funds on track.

Points to remember

1. Asset allocation describes the splitting of your money between different stock markets, sectors and styles.

2. Keep an open mind; don't rigidly follow one particular type of asset allocation to the exclusion of others.

3. There is considerable professional debate about whether it is possible to asset allocate successfully.

4. In general the fund management industry hugs its variety of benchmarks too closely.

5. Investors should be interested in absolute risk, not how closely their funds match what others are doing.

6. Volatility is not the same thing as risk, and the difference between them creates opportunities for smart investors.

Jupiter Merlin in action

"Uncertainty and expectation are the joys of life."
William Congreve

What the fund does

As an example of how my team at Jupiter invests in funds, I am going to use the Jupiter Merlin Growth Portfolio. We perceive it as a 'one-stop shop' for a UK based investor who wants a diversified portfolio exposed to the opportunities available in equity markets across the world, but who doesn't want all his investments outside the UK. Some people use it as a 'core' portfolio before adding other favourites of theirs around the edges; but in many ways, not least the taxation advantages of the capital gains tax position (whereby the profits on any sales we make within the fund are not taxable), if you are happy with it as a concept and us as investors, there is no need to look further.

The general philosophy we adopt follows closely the steps I have outlined in previous chapters. The stages are:

1. Review the general investment climate;
2. Decide on an appropriate asset allocation;
3. Select the funds that are most likely to do well in the current investment climate; and
4. Monitor the resulting portfolios on a daily basis.

In practice, because we have been studying fund managers that we know well for many years, it is only occasionally that we move outside the circle of the 50 or so managers whom we judge to be the best in their particular field (though we spend a lot of time looking for new talent coming through).

The main way in which we adjust our portfolios is by changing our percentage holdings in individual funds. There are, however, occasions (such as March 2003) when we feel the markets have reached an important turning point and on those occasions we may change the composition of our portfolio quite dramatically, bringing in new funds with a style or regional focus that matches our world view, and dropping those that no longer fit the bill. This does not mean that we think the fund managers in question have suddenly become bad managers, merely that the markets in our view are entering a period when their type of fund will not do so well.

The fund of funds concept

Jupiter Merlin Growth Portfolio's structure is that of a fund of funds. As such it has slightly higher fees than a standard unit trust; my view on this subject is that we have to show better than average performance, after fees, otherwise the fund is not worth investing in. I am glad to report that so far we have achieved this goal (see Appendix 1). It currently operates under the CIS (Collective Investment Scheme) rules (see Glossary), with the stated aim "To achieve long-term capital growth"; its investment policy is "To invest in unit trusts, OEICs and other regulated collective investment schemes across several management groups. The underlying funds invest in equities and fixed interest stocks across different geographical areas with a core in the UK". The Jupiter Merlin Growth Portfolio sits in the IMA Active Managed Sector and therefore must have at least 10% invested in non-UK equities and is allowed to invest up to 100% in equities. The one other limitation we keep to, other than the CIS rules for fund of funds unit trusts, is that we don't have more than 25% invested in other Jupiter unit trusts (which, however, you could regard as a 'secret weapon' as they are free to us).

It is worth mentioning that the CIS rules primarily prevent us from having more than 20% of our portfolio in any one underlying fund. I remember having a problem with this rule in 2002, as our more cautious income fund had a large weighting in a gilt index tracker at the time. As the stock markets fell sharply in July 2002, this holding not only kept edging up in price, it also kept breaking the 20% barrier as the other constituents fell every day. Undoubtedly it was not a high risk holding, but the combination of volatile markets and strict rules certainly kept us on our toes. The other technical point to mention is that Jupiter Merlin Growth is allowed to buy offshore funds as well as onshore unit trusts, which widens the choice of funds open to us.

The fund's investment policy is to have its core holdings in the UK markets. At the end of October 2005, the fund had 25.7% invested directly in UK funds, while a couple of our specialist sector investments also owned some UK shares. We know roughly how much extra UK exposure we have from this source (approximately 6%), but the exact figure is not something that we monitor closely. This harks back to my point in the last chapter about what sort of asset allocation 'process' one should use. Ours does not require us to operate within set limits. If you look back over the years, you will see that at times this fund has had as much as 70% invested in the UK. As you might imagine, that implies that we are not that enthused about the UK as an investment area at the moment. Why is that?

Jupiter Merlin Growth Portfolio Fund

Holdings as at 31st October 2005 (names of managers in brackets)

UK	25.7%	Artemis UK Special Situations (Derek Stuart)
		Fidelity Special Situations (Anthony Bolton)
		Framlington UK Smaller Companies (Roger Whiteoak)
		Framlington UK Select Opportunities (Nigel Thomas)
		GAM UK Diversified (Andrew Green)
		Merrill Lynch UK Dynamic (Mark Lyttleton)
USA	16.6%	Findlay Park US Smaller Companies (James Findlay & Charlie Park)
Europe	5.5%	Artemis European Growth (Philip Wolstencroft)
		Jupiter European (Alex Darwall)
Japan	16.1%	CF Morant Wright Japan (Ian Wright & Stephen Morant)
		Melchior Japan Opportunities (Ken Nishizawa)
Asia	1.7%	Lincoln Far East (Liz Desmond)
Specialist	34.4%	Investec GS Global Energy (Tim Guinness)
		JP Morgan Natural Resources (Ian Henderson)
		Jupiter Financial Opportunities (Philip Gibbs)
		Jupiter Emerging European Opportunities (Elena Shaftan)
		M&G Global Basics (Graham French)
Cash	0%	Cash
Total	100%	

UK investments

The answer relates to the way that the UK economy is structured and to some of the trends that have been apparent since 2001. One of the key differences between the UK and Continental Europe is that the UK has a much higher proportion (around 70%) of home owners. Added to that, most houses in this country are financed by mortgages that have repayments linked to short-term interest rates. This means that there is significant sensitivity in the economy to movements in the Bank of England's base rate.

Base rates have been falling in a long-term trend since the peak of 17% in 1980. In those days, interest rates had to move quite large amounts in nominal terms in order to have the desired effect on economic behaviour. More recently, as inflation has fallen, so too have nominal interest rates, to a low of 3.5% in November 2003. Since then, the Bank of England has raised short-term interest rates five times in 0.25% moves to a peak of 4.75% that lasted a year from August 2004 to August 2005, before reducing them slightly to their current level of 4.5%.

This is not, you might think, a massive change; but in reality it means that interest rates increased by 28%, as have most people's monthly mortgage payments. In the earlier decades, this would have been the equivalent of raising base rates from 8.5% to 11%. Many people have mortgages whose interest rates are only changed once each year, so it takes time for them to notice the effect of changes in interest rates. The combination of increased mortgage repayments, increases in energy prices and continuing rises in council tax (mine has increased by 100.5% with no change in circumstances since 1st April 1997) has ensured that consumer spending has been held in check.

We have also had a view for over a year that the rate of increase in house prices was unsustainable, and that they would, in due course, start to fall. This has undoubtedly started to happen, but the full consequences are unlikely to be played out in full for two or three years. People have very short memories – think back to 1989-93, which saw five years of falling house prices in the UK, or for that matter, what happened to Japanese house prices from 1990 to 2004, when average house prices fell by around 80%. What we are seeing in the UK at the moment is a decline in the number of housing transactions, at a time when prices have started to fall. At some stage, the volume of transactions should pick up, but prices will have to fall for the market to clear, which will lead to further effects on consumer spending.

As a team, we think that the weakness in the private sector has been hidden from view by the vast increases in public spending since the re-election of the Labour Government in 2001, when the brakes were well and truly taken off the Government spending machine. The consequence of all this is that we have tended to find more attractive areas in the world to invest in, and where we have UK funds, we have tried to use managers who agree with our view of the UK economic situation, and who therefore have portfolios biased towards companies whose earnings derive from overseas markets rather than the domestic scene.

The list of funds shows you the names of the holdings, and given the amount that is written about them, I don't think that Derek Stuart, Anthony Bolton (see the excellent book 'Investing with Anthony Bolton'), Nigel Thomas, Roger Whiteoak, Andrew Green or Mark Lyttleton need much introduction from me. Suffice it to say that they are all experienced investors. In particular, Anthony, Nigel and Andrew have all been managing money for over 20 years, and have seen virtually everything that the market can throw at them. All investors can have more difficult patches, as Andrew Green has had recently (certainly compared to his own high standards). However we believe that you don't go from being a good investor to being a bad one overnight, and have therefore kept money with him, albeit at a slightly reduced weighting for the present.

On the other hand, we are very happy with our high conviction weighting in Anthony Bolton's Fidelity Special Situations Fund despite the media frenzy regarding his succession plans. As we see it, Anthony is one of the most perceptive investors around, has the wind behind him, and we have the opportunity to have money managed by him for two more years. Even then, he will not want to pass his mantle on to fund managers not up to the job, and we do have the chance to change our mind if we don't like what we see. It doesn't seem to be one of the more difficult decisions that we have to make.

Opportunities overseas

But where are those opportunities overseas? The United States of America has to be the first port of call; it is the largest, most vibrant economy in the world and opportunities abound there for wealth creation. Having said that, it is also the market that fund managers find it most difficult to beat, probably because it is more researched by more people than any other in the world. It is hard to find consistently good performance in UK unit trusts investing in the United States. Going back to 1999/2000, it was also a market that had more technology companies than most other markets, and many US fund managers felt the need to own some of these companies, however outrageous their valuations were.

As I mentioned in Chapter Five, I had the fortune to come across James Findlay in 1992, where he was running the F&C US Smaller Companies Fund. He used value principles and had no direct investments in technology. I invested money with him then and we followed him to Findlay Park in 1998 when he set up an offshore OEIC (based in Dublin), which thankfully, is FSA recognised (and therefore an allowable investment in a fund of funds). His fund is our only exposure to the US market, and as you can see, it is a healthy 16.6%.

Some people would say that is an overly large and 'risky' position. Our view is that it is precisely the opposite. We see James as a very talented, experienced investor who, with Charlie Park and the excellent team that he has built up around him, has the ability to generate considerably above average returns for our investors, combined with a below average probability of losing money. As a team, we try to look at what we see is the likelihood of a particular fund manager losing us money before we explore the upside potential. If we find an investor who fits the bill, we will allocate money to him, the proportion depending upon our level of conviction. As you might imagine, we have a high level of conviction in James' team at Findlay Park.

Whilst discussing the US, one other point worth bringing out is that of currency. Investment overseas brings with it currency exposure, which can either make or lose you money, depending on whether the foreign currency is, respectively, strong or weak against sterling. For most of the last four years, the US dollar has been weak against most major currencies, and for some of that time, in order to save our investors money we had a currency hedge in place on our dollar holdings. Our current view (and all our views are subject to change at short notice!) is that the US dollar, which has been strengthening in 2005, will continue to be stronger whilst the Federal Reserve continues to raise interest rates. When they are seen to have stopped, the dollar may then start to weaken again.

As a sterling investor, you also have to think about what might happen to our own currency, and our current view is that it is likely to be weak as a result of all the factors discussed above about the UK economy. If both the dollar and sterling are weak, you then have to decide which is likely to be weaker! For the record, Edward Bonham Carter, Jupiter's Chief Investment Officer, thinks that successfully trading currencies is very hard and probably not worth worrying about in the long-term. We agree to differ on this point, but there is no doubt that forecasting currencies is extremely difficult. As a team, we will only hedge a currency if we have a very strong view. Otherwise we accept the currency exposure that overseas investment brings.

The potential in Japan

An area that we have become increasingly optimistic about over the last couple of years has been Japan. The Japanese stock market has, with odd exceptions, consistently lost investors money since 1990. However we feel that with property prices now on the rise, the reduction in cross-shareholdings between Japanese companies and the re-election of Prime Minister Koizumi with a reforming mandate, investors in Japanese shares will make good money over the next few years. We have actually been able to make a 90% return (so far) with our investment in the CF Morant Wright Japan fund, run by Ian Wright and Stephen Morant, since our investment in their new unit trust in May 2003. The recent past has been kind, but we think there is more to go for.

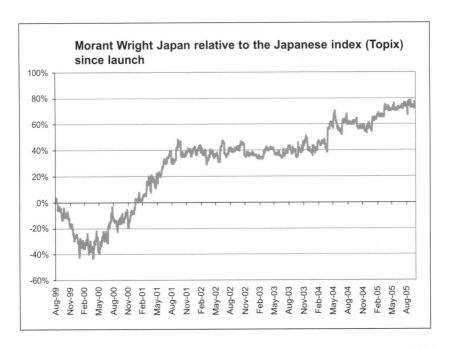

Morant Wright Japan relative to the Japanese index (Topix) since launch

Source: Lipper, total return in GBP to 30th September 2005

Morant Wright is a firm set up in a very similar way to Findlay Park. Stephen Morant was a partner at the blue-chip stockbroking firm Cazenove, while Ian Wright used to manage the Japanese portion of Foreign & Colonial Investment Trust. The two joined forces to set up their boutique fund management company in 1999. They had spotted an anomaly in that many small and mid-sized Japanese shares had share prices well below their book value, which they thought could be profitably exploited. You could therefore categorise them as value investors, an approach we feel very comfortable with in this market. As we have increased our commitment to Japan, we have also started an investment in Melchior Japan Opportunities, run by Ken Nishizawa, a fund manager who also 'fishes' in the pool of companies below the very largest. He, however, puts more of an emphasis on growth than value, a fact that has been to his advantage more latterly as the reality of Japan's recovery becomes more widely recognised.

Specialist holdings

So far we have discussed the 'geographical' overseas holdings, but as you can see, the fund holds around a third of its investments in what we describe as 'Specialist' or 'Other' holdings. There are really three themes running through here. Firstly, emerging markets seem to us to be where the real growth in the world is, and rather than buying a generalist fund that covers every emerging market that exists, we feel that it is right to pick out the most attractive region.

To us, that means Eastern Europe, where share prices are attractive, and where we at Jupiter are lucky enough to have Elena Shaftan, with Ingrid Kukuljan, running the top performing unit trust in this area. In fact as a fund of funds team, we were instrumental in helping this fund to see the light of day, not only being substantial initial investors on day one, but also arguing the case for having it beforehand. Elena is Russian, Ingrid comes from Croatia, and we think that in these markets where the background is different to that of many Western countries, it is important to have someone who understands the mindset of local investors and politicians.

This was particularly important when the 'Yukos affair' was running its course. If you remember, the Western press castigated the Kremlin for arresting Mikhail Khordokovsky, and said that it heralded the demise of Russian capitalism. The 'Russian' view on the other hand, which we learnt from Elena, was rather more prosaic: the man had 'stolen' assets from the Russian state. He had also not kept to his side of the 'keep out of politics and we won't interfere in your companies' bargain, and was therefore paying the price. Without making a judgement about the rights and wrongs of the situation, we felt that the Russian view would prevail, and therefore kept our exposure to the area and the fund, which turned out to be the correct decision. Anyone who had believed the Western financial press would almost certainly have removed any investment they had there, thus depriving themselves of considerable returns since then.

Our specialist holdings also include three funds that are part of the theme related to rising resource and energy prices, of which Russia is also a beneficiary. We have been investors in this sector for three years now, based on research that has led us to believe the following:

- Demand for oil from Western countries is relatively inelastic in the short-term;
- Global economic growth will continue to be reasonable;
- Demand from fast growing countries such as China and India will continue to grow;
- Global oil output is close to its maximum in the near-term; and
- There are supply bottlenecks in oil refining.

People have been talking about the idea of a 'bubble' in the energy sector. Although prices have risen sharply, short-term and momentum investors are probably involved and periodic pullbacks are inevitable, it does seem to us to be a trend that is sustainable. Global growth is good, there are plenty of 'unbelievers' and valuations are still reasonable.

Investec GS Global Energy (our second offshore fund) is run by Tim Guinness, one of the founders of Guinness Flight, a firm that was bought by Investec in 1998. He invests in companies that are benefiting from the rise in the oil price. All bar 3% of the fund have a market capitalisation of over $1bn, and if the price of oil stays above $55 per barrel (which we think is likely) his portfolio is on a P/E for 2005 earnings of under twelve times.

The reasons for owning the funds run by Ian Henderson (JPM Natural Resources) and Graham French (M&G Global Basics) are similar. We are trying to buy in to the dynamics of rising raw material prices, but spreading our 'bets' in what is a very volatile sector, and making sure that we have enough exposure to the larger companies that have cash flows and profits as well as some of the smaller exploration stocks where there can be great upside, but also considerable scope for disappointment (Regal Petroleum was a good recent example of this).

Finally, the holding of Philip Gibbs' Jupiter Financial Opportunities fund is also in the specialist sector. Here we have a prime example of a holding in a fund because of the fund manager rather than the sector. We don't have a particular view about whether financials in general are a good bet, but we do know that our colleague Philip is an exceptional investor. His fund's price has gone up from 50p at launch to around 270p at the time of writing, a fivefold rise and one making it the best performing unit trust over that period by some considerable margin. I first came across the name Philip Gibbs in the early 1990s when he was the top-rated financials analyst for seven years in a row in the Extel survey. It was clear then, reading his research, that he was one of the few people who understood the dynamics of companies and their share prices, thought for himself and was prepared to speak his mind rather than follow the herd. His unit trust is a reflection of those attributes.

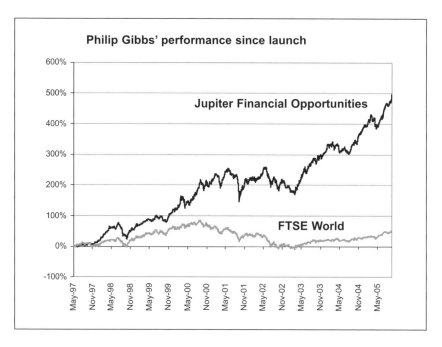

Source: Lipper total return in GBP to 30th September 2005

How the fund has changed

Looking back over the last few years, it is interesting to see in what ways the make-up of Jupiter Merlin Growth has changed and what has stayed constant. Over the last three years, we have managed to get the major themes right; plenty of smaller company exposure across the world, nothing in larger

US companies, good exposure to emerging markets and resources, and an increasing amount invested in Japan. What has changed is that up until March 2003, we had a very defensive portfolio, whereas since the 13th March 2003 we have been on the front foot, driven by an increasing conviction that we were in a bull market. The crystal ball is never that clear and so I cannot predict with any certainty what the future will bring. What I can predict is that we will be watching events closely, and be ready to alter our portfolios if we feel that conditions have fundamentally altered.

I hope that this chapter has given you a feel for how I and my team choose our investments although there are some funds and areas that I have missed out for the sake of brevity, specifically Asia-ex Japan and Europe. Overall, the key points I would emphasise are these:

- We use our experience and screening systems to make sure we identify (and get to know) the best fund managers in each of the main fund and market sectors.

- Our process begins, however, with a view of the current investment climate. This drives our asset allocation decisions and also the style of the funds that we are currently looking for.

- It is only once we have decided on the right amount of money to have in each of the main regions, and the style we think appropriate, that we pick the funds we want in each of the portfolios we run.

- When we find a fund manager that we feel particularly confident about (such as an Anthony Bolton or a James Findlay) we may choose to stick with them for a long period of time.

- We take little notice of how the weightings in our fund compare, either with what the average fund in our sector is doing, or with the composition of the benchmark we are measured against.

- In some cases, and particularly with specialist funds, we are happy to back a fund manager whose talents we have come to admire, regardless of whether we have strong views about their particular area of expertise.

Fund management is a people business, as I have said before, and that runs right through the composition of our fund. The funds we own are all run by individuals we know well and trust. At the same time we endeavour to structure our portfolio so that it reflects our broader view of the world. There are always some decisions that investors need to make for themselves, and these big picture decisions fall into that category. Unfortunately you cannot usually pick the best funds and leave it at that. It is important to point out that we want all the positions in our portfolio to be 'working hard' and that if one is not and we have a better idea, then the better idea will be included instead. Aside from these principles, there are other characteristics of the portfolio that are the result of lessons learnt over the years, which I would like to share with you before I close.

Points to remember

1. Funds of funds offer investors the chance to let a professional investor pick the best fund managers on their behalf.

2. Jupiter's Merlin Growth Portfolio is a global fund that is unconstrained by sector and geographical restrictions, though the core holdings are in the UK.

3. The UK economy is likely to perform relatively poorly in 2006 and beyond because of its housing market bias, rising Government spending and other factors.

4. It is difficult to find funds sold in the UK that do consistently well in the United States' market.

5. Japan and emerging markets are set to do relatively well in the future.

6. Energy and resource companies still look good value.

10

The secrets of success

"Enjoy failure and learn from it. You never learn from success."

James Dyson

"My formula for success is rise early, work late and strike oil."

John Paul Getty

"I keep six honest serving-men
(They taught me all I knew);
Their names are What and Why and When
And How and Where and Who."

Rudyard Kipling

The need for humility

I'm not sure that I completely agree with the quote from James Dyson, but I do understand the sentiment. You cannot have been in the investment business for fifteen years without having made some real howlers and there is no doubt that you should never stop learning; but I do hope that I have learnt from things we have got right as well as from the mistakes. I have included some of the hard-learnt lessons here in the hope that they will help you become a better investor.

As an investor, it is important to have a positive frame of mind, while accepting that you will not get it right 100% of the time. In fact, as I mentioned in Chapter five, one of the most important lessons I have learnt is that many of the best investors can make an investment for all the right reasons and then suddenly, realise that either something fundamental has changed, or they have made a mistake and, rather than agonising about it for days, cut the position, probably at a loss, and invest the money somewhere else. Often this will be in an investment that is 'facing' in completely the opposite direction.

This 'intellectual humility', if you will, is a fair indicator of a good investor. You also need the confidence to move on and then believe in your own competence to make the next investment decision. This is not, of course, to be confused with intellectual arrogance. Experience gives you a feel for which type of investor you have in front of you.

The lessons of youth

My early years in managing portfolios of funds were spent at what was then called Henderson Administration plc, now known as Henderson Global Investors. It was in their tender arms that I cut my teeth, and I have much to thank them for, particularly as they gave me the opportunity to manage money. When I look back at the make-up of the portfolios I ran then, they were too diversified for my tastes now in terms of the number of funds they held, and they were often too timid in their approach.

There seemed to be a culture there that did not encourage junior fund managers to 'express themselves in their portfolios', I think as a result of the painful experiences generated by the 1987 crash and its aftermath, which destroyed liquidity in smaller companies and hurt Henderson's performance at the time. As it happens, the culture probably saved me (and my clients) from myself, but it was quite frustrating to see what could be done but wasn't.

On the point about diversification within the Jupiter Merlin Growth Portfolio, although there are only seventeen funds in the list, underlying them are some 1,000 different shares. A portfolio that consists of that number of shares is certainly diversified in terms of single company risk. If owning 1,000 shares allows a fund to achieve above average performance, how many is too many? As with many investment questions, there is no one right answer, and it would depend on whether the holdings were concentrated in one sector or one country.

One of the largest number of holdings I came across was in a 'cautious managed' fund. It had 4,397 individual stocks in its portfolio – and that was just for the 13.5% equity portion of the £49m fund. The average holding size was just £1,504! It was obviously part of a larger sum of money being run on a 'model' basis with the help of computers. My observation is that the manager was almost certainly diversifying to such an extent that any chance of above average performance was remote. In fact, it is likely that particular multi-manager fund was, in effect, an expensive index-tracker. In my team, we have certainly learnt to keep our portfolios focussed and concentrated in order to do the best for our clients. Performance has improved over the years as a result.

Many of the lessons I learnt at Henderson concerned the technicalities of unit trusts and the dynamics of an asset management business. I learnt why forward pricing was so important, for example, from a brush with a canny investor in a range of life funds. He proved very adept at exploiting the fact that at the time these funds were all valued on an 'historic pricing' basis. So, the prices investors were quoted were based on an earlier valuation point (often the previous day's price), rather than the next day's 'forward price'. We eventually stopped what he was up to by moving from historic to forward pricing, but not before he had made a large amount of money, dealing with the certainty of hindsight, at the expense of the other life fund holders. This was at a time well before the phrase 'market timing' held any resonance for fund management groups.

I also learnt that the administrative structure of a product is vital. To keep investors happy, you need to create a fund that is not only capable of being 'scaled up' in size, but that will also remain manageable from an administration point of view. Managing individual portfolios for clients tends to be an 'admin-heavy' business. As a result, you tend to end up spending more effort making sure that the administrative structure works, and less time choosing the best investments.

This is the reason why my team now only runs funds of funds. Our aim is to provide strong performance for every investor in each fund. A unit trust structure, with its emphasis on equality of treatment for every individual investor, is undoubtedly the most efficient way to do this. To see why this is so, you need to imagine how you would run a model portfolio for more than 5,000 individual clients, which is what we were doing towards the end of my time at Lazard Asset Management. Every time one of these investors decided to add more money to their portfolio, we had to buy new units just for them. The same thing happened in reverse when an investor decided to withdraw some money. With that many individual portfolios, it meant we were both buying and selling small amounts of funds every day of the week! Even with excellent computer systems, such a process can easily create an administrative nightmare.

Alternatively, if every client's portfolio is different, how can you provide assurance to your investors that they are all benefiting from your best ideas? The answer is that you cannot. With a fund of funds, this problem is averted. Investors can easily see that they are getting equal treatment. A well run fund of funds does the same job as an individual portfolio service, like the one we had at Lazard, but with considerably less administrative complexity. The structure is also more tax efficient and more transparent. While running individual portfolios is fine in theory, in practice more often than not such a service panders to the egos of the clients (who like the sound of the idea that they are getting bespoke treatment) rather than helping them fulfil their real investment needs.

Look at the valuation

In the autumn of 1998 whilst I was working at Lazard, many shares were very cheap as a result of the Russian default crisis. We owned a position in the HSBC UK Smaller Companies Fund, which we had bought at launch in September 1996. This had made good positive returns for our clients, even after the effects of the crisis; it also performed much better than both the smaller company indices and averages, and also the FTSE All Share Index.

Around that time, the lead manager of the fund, Ashton Bradbury, resigned to go to another job, and was replaced, though only after a couple of months, by David Taylor whom we didn't meet. Now I have already argued that fund management is a people business, so you may be surprised that we took the decision to sell the fund without meeting the new manager or doing enough research. With hindsight, we should have been much more diligent.

At the time, UK smaller companies were about as cheap as they had ever been, which we would have realised had we bothered to stop and think about it. We should have kept that bit of money as a smaller companies holding. It wouldn't have made much difference to performance whether we had kept the original fund, or followed Ashton to his new fund. But the worst decision was the one that we did make and that was to move the money into a more general UK fund. Even though it did beat the FTSE All Share Index, it did not do as well as either of the smaller companies funds would have done had we gone with them.

The important lesson from this episode is that you should look very carefully at the valuations of the shares and sectors underlying any fund you are thinking of buying or selling, to gauge the level of opportunity and the downside risk. Valuation, that is to say whether the investments are cheap or expensive, really does matter. The other lesson from this rather painful mistake is that it is important to do your homework before you make or dispose of an investment.

Think for yourselves

The quote that I used at the beginning of the second chapter from George Bernard Shaw is one well worth taking to heart; it suggests that most people don't think for themselves. As an individual investor, you certainly should. Independence of thought is something that should be encouraged within fund management groups as well. Not all of them have the right culture. I remember well at an investment meeting in the mid 1990s giving a rather facile example (it was bitumen paint!) of how the price of some goods appeared to be going down, and being laughed out of court.

As it turned out, the relentless march of disinflation was one of the key drivers of share prices through much of that decade, but at the time it was not a commonly held view. I didn't have the confidence to take it any further and I had certainly not helped my cause with the example I used. It has made me try to listen properly to people's ideas, even if they do not have much experience, rather than ignoring them. You never know where your next good idea may come from!

Another secret of success

Some years ago, I met a very successful man who told me one of the secrets of his success. He had not been born with the proverbial silver spoon in his mouth, nor had he a large inheritance. However, when he left school, he sat down and worked out what sort of lifestyle he would like to have, what sort of house he wanted to live in, what he wanted to do in his spare time and so on and then proceeded to work out how much his aspirations were going to cost. He then decided at what age he would like to retire, and therefore how many years he would be working.

From that, he calculated the number of working months, weeks, days, and finally hours he would have available, and therefore the amount he needed to earn each and every hour in order to fulfil his aspirations. He was, and is, a very energetic man, and needless to say he achieved all of his targets and more, within the time he had allotted.

Liquidity matters

One of the many mistakes I have made relates to liquidity in markets, and will, I am sure, resonate with most professional investors. In the mid 1990s I was trying to sell a block of income shares of an investment trust. Having asked our dealers to see what the options were, they came back to me with the news that they had found a buyer. He was offering me a choice: either to buy half my holding at the quoted bid price on the screen, the rest to be done 'as and when'. Or he would buy the whole block, but for 2% less. I chose the first option, only to see the price fall further as soon as I had got rid of the first half. We failed to sell the other half for more than two weeks, and only then at a very much lower price.

If you have something to sell in what you consider to be an illiquid market (houses, by the way, can often come into this category), my advice is that "a bird in the hand is worth two in the bush". Illiquid markets can make a fool of all of us, and accepting a discount on the quoted price today is usually cheaper than haggling over the pennies in the long run. Luckily as an investor in funds, you are unlikely to come across this situation unless circumstances are extreme, but you may do so in property over the next couple of years.

Property (unsurprisingly) was the underlying investment for the Prime Residential Property Fund, launched in the mid 1980s. It was a very popular fund, available through a life fund 'wrapper'. The investment story was that top-end residential properties in London were increasing faster in price than anywhere else in the country, but the majority of private investors could not afford to buy these properties, as many were valued at over £1m. A fund seemed to be the perfect answer, as it allowed anyone with £1,000 to participate. Performance was good up until August 1988, at which point the residential property market in the UK started to fall in response to rising interest rates.

Canny investors took their money and profits early, but it was not long before investors started to take their money out faster than the fund could sell its houses and flats. Liquidity in the property market was drying up. The small print of the fund's constitution allowed those running the fund to impose a twelve month moratorium on people taking money out in order to protect the investors who remained, and that is indeed what happened. This created uproar amongst investors and advisers, but it was a fair way of dealing with the situation, and should not have been a surprise given what was happening in the property market in general.

The lessons that I take from this (although it was not a situation that I was directly involved in) are:

- You should always determine the liquidity of the investments in any fund that you buy;

- When you invest in a fund that itself invests in relatively illiquid assets, you should know what the potential downside is;

- This means not only considering the odds of the price going down, but also what could happen if you are not allowed to sell when you want to; and

- Once you have decided that you need to sell an investment, it is usually better to sell too early rather than too late.

Mistakes we all make

Finally, I think it would be instructive to look at what I consider to be the three key mistakes I have observed fund investors to make. I am not claiming to have been immune from making any of them in the past, but we, in my team, all carry these around in our heads as "number one things not to do"!

1. Confusing risk with volatility. There is no doubt in my mind that many investors, both professional and private, dislike volatility (as we saw earlier). Nirvana, for them, is an investment that climbs upwards, exhibiting below average levels of volatility whilst performing in an above average manner. As the fairy tale says: "And they all lived happily ever after." My view is that over any sensible time frame share based investments, which are essentially investments in continued economic growth and prosperity, will make you considerably more money than cash or fixed interest based ones. However during that journey, there will be ups and downs as sentiment and interest rates rise and fall.

Unfortunately, many people consider the volatility exhibited to be risk; as you have seen, I think that real risk is the probability of losing your money in total. People say that "change creates opportunity", and in my view, so does volatility. There are indeed investments that have fewer peaks and troughs, but do not expect them to make as high a return. And look very carefully at the mechanism from which the lack of volatility is derived from. If it appears to be too good to be true, it probably is, as some investors in with-profits funds, amongst others, have discovered to their cost. Examine yourself, and work out whether you wish to maximise your returns, or minimise the volatility of your investments.

2. Extrapolating the past into the future. As I said earlier, I think that the past performance of an individual fund manager can give you clues as to how he is likely to perform in the future. It is one thing to say that, but it is quite another to imagine that what has just happened is likely to continue happening ad infinitum. Unfortunately it seems to be human nature to do just that. As the sheep in the front cover cartoon suggests, most people like to be doing what everyone else is. So the moral has to be: be brave. Be (an informed) contrarian.

3. Buying at the top and selling at the bottom. This is related to the second point, in that by the time the least well-informed investor has heard about the latest 'dead cert' investment, it is almost certainly too late. The canny investors are selling their investments on to the unsuspecting 'mug punters'. The final stages of the technology boom showed this sort of behaviour, when people, often those who really couldn't afford to, invested far too much of their savings in investments that subsequently fell over 80%. Similarly, when the phrase "abandon hope all ye who enter here" springs to mind, it is a good bet that the worst is over and that the most profitable thing to do will be, at the very least, to hang on in there, and possibly even add some more money to the investment. This requires psychological 'bravery' and probably some patience as well.

Final thoughts

At the risk of repeating myself one more time, the most important lesson I have learnt is that people are what make the difference in fund management. There are a few very good ones around, though not that many exceptional ones. Investment is an art not a science.

In summary, having read this book, I hope that you will agree with me on the need to sort out your financial objectives, put in some investigative work, read well and widely, try to decide what the future holds and buy good fund managers who you expect to do well in that environment. In other words, buy the right amounts of the right people, at the right time! Put that way, it sounds very simple, but that is not to say that it is easy. Good luck!

Points to remember

1. Don't become emotionally attached to any investment.

2. Don't over-diversify your investments.

3. Look carefully at the valuation of the shares underlying a fund.

4. Think for yourself, and laterally.

5. Liquidity matters.

6. People matter most of all.

Glossary

Administration	When a company becomes insolvent, but rather than be broken up in bankruptcy, it is refinanced as a going concern, eventually being rehabilitated as a public company.
Alpha	The value added by a fund manager after stripping out the effects of the market (beta).
Arithmetic Index	An index calculated by using simple (i.e. added or subtracted) returns from its components.
Beta	The value added to or subtracted from a portfolio by the market, and therefore its sensitivity to the market. i.e. If a fund has a beta of more than 1, you would expect it to go up faster than a rising market (and go down faster than a falling one).
Bid basis	The pricing basis of a unit trust when there are more sellers of the fund than there are buyers.
Bid/Selling Price	The price an investor receives when selling a unit trust. Can be the same as the cancellation price, but is not necessarily so – see Chapter three.
Bloomberg	Commercial provider of historic and real-time data, including that of funds.
Bond	Fixed interest loan instrument
Cancellation Price	The lowest price an investor selling a unit trust can receive, usually used if the units are being cancelled rather than sold on to another investor.
CIS	Collective Investment Schemes sourcebook – the previous source for the rules governing open-ended funds.

COLL	The new Collective Investment Scheme Sourcebook, introduced by the FSA in April 2004; it will fully replace CIS on 12th February 2007.
Corporate Bond	Fixed interest instrument loan issued by a company.
CPI	Consumer Prices Index – the new common measure of inflation, harmonised across the EU, which excludes, amongst other things, rises in council tax and mortgage repayments.
Derivative	A financial instrument. Its performance is linked to (derived from) the performance of the share/bond/currency etc that it is based upon.
Dilution Levy	A levy of approximately 1% on the purchase and sale of a fund, being payable into the fund's assets. It is the alternative means whereby a single priced fund can avoid the dilution of its remaining holders by large deals in and out of the fund.
Forward Pricing	Funds are usually priced 'forward' i.e. in the future, at a set time. Investors place their deals to buy or sell not knowing what exact price they will be dealing at, unlike with historic pricing.
Full Offer Price	The highest price payable to buy a unit trust, which includes the full initial charge.
Geometric Index	An index calculated by using compounded (i.e. multiplied or divided) returns from its components.

Historic Pricing	Once the norm, most funds are not priced this way now. Funds were priced at a set time, and then investors were allowed to deal at that price until the next valuation point. Investors were essentially being allowed to deal with the benefit of hindsight, often to the detriment of existing unitholders.
Holding	The amount of units that you own in a fund (or a fund owns in shares). E.g. The fund's holding in Jupiter Income, or Jupiter Income's position in BP. Interchangeable with 'position'.
IMA	Investment Management Association – trade body of UK investment managers.
Index	A mathematical formulation, made up of a number of shares, created to measure the performance of a stock market or sub-sector of a market.
Index Tracker	A fund aiming to mimic the performance of the index that it is chosen to track.
Information Ratio	A measure of relative value added per unit of relative risk taken. Normal formula for calculation = Return – Benchmark Return / Tracking Error.
Investment Trust	Closed-ended investment vehicle, structured under UK Company Law. Price in the market is determined by supply and demand.
IPO	Initial Public Offering. The US nomenclature for a new issue.
ISA	Individual Savings Account – successor to the PEP (and almost identical) – Tax free wrapper in which unit trusts, OEICs and shares can be placed.

Lipper	Commercial provider of historic data including that of funds.
Liquidity	a) The colloquial term for cash – aka "I have 8% liquidity within my fund".
	b) The depth of a market. If a market is 'highly liquid', it is possible to buy or sell much larger quantities than in one that is 'less liquid'.
Logarithmic chart	A chart which measures the rate of change in the data being presented, rather than just the absolute change shown in a linear graph.
Mutual Fund	US name for a vehicle similar to a unit trust or OEIC.
NAV	Net Asset Value – the pro-rata value of assets ascribed to each share of an OEIC or investment trust. Not usually used in connection with a unit trust, but the true mid-price of a unit trust could be described as its NAV.
New Issue	The issue of shares in a company to the public, via a market, for the first time.
OEIC	Open Ended Investment Company, structured under company law. Priced using underlying NAV.
Offer basis	The pricing basis of a unit trust when there are more buyers of the fund than there are sellers.
Offer/Buying Price	The price an investor pays to buy a unit trust, which may or may not be the full offer price – see Chapter three.
Offshore fund	Funds that are not domiciled in the UK. Those that are FSA recognised, and therefore more readily available in the UK tend to be based in Dublin, Luxembourg or the Channel Islands. Not all offshore funds are FSA recognised; you

can find out by looking at their prices in the *Financial Times* where contact details such as address and telephone number, are only given for FSA recognised funds. Alternatively you can check with the fund management group whose fund it is.

Onshore fund	Funds that are based (and therefore regulated) in the UK.
Par	The face value of a fixed interest bond, usually £100.
PEP	'Personal Equity Plan' – tax free wrapper in which unit trusts, OEICs and shares can be placed.
P/E	Price/Earnings ratio – a measure of how expensive a share is; compares the current price to either the historic or the prospective earnings per share of the company.
Real Return	The percentage return from an investment after deducting the rate of inflation from its actual percentage return.
Redemption Yield	The yield to maturity of a fixed interest instrument – takes account of any capital erosion if the price is above par.
Relative Return Graph	A pictorial view of how a fund is doing relative to the chosen comparison. When the relative line moves up the fund is out-performing. When the line moves down, it is under-performing.
Returns Based Analysis	Analysis of fund price movements to determine the style and value added of a fund manager.

RPI	Retail Prices Index – until recently, the most commonly used measure of inflation in the UK, and the one still used in index-linked gilts. Superseded by the EU 'harmonised' CPI in Government communications.
Sharpe Ratio	A measure of absolute value added per unit of absolute risk. The formula = Return – Risk free rate (e.g. interest rate on cash) / Standard deviation of the return.
Single Price	The single price of an open-ended investment company. Not all that it seems, as it can often be varied depending on whether the fund is creating shares (units) or redeeming. The latter is known as a 'swinging single price', which has the same effect as the dual price of a unit trust, thereby avoiding the dilution of its shareholders.
SIPP	Self Invested Personal Pension. Individual pension wrapper, usually for higher earners.
Sovereign Bond	Fixed interest loan instrument issued by a Government or quasi-governmental organisation.
Spread	The difference between the price you buy a fund at, and the price that you can sell it at.
SSAS	Small Self Administered Scheme – type of pension fund no longer created, similar to a SIPP, but many still in existence.
Stock Lending	The practice of lending out shares or bonds from a portfolio (usually by long-term holders) in return for some extra income. Those borrowing the stock are likely to be 'shorting' it in expectation of it's price going down. The income from stock lending can be compared to interest received from lending out money.

Tracking Error	A measure of relative 'risk'. The percentage per year that a portfolio is likely to out or under-perform an index at a 95% probability level, i.e. in 95 cases out of 100.
Turn	The profit a market-maker makes from buying a share at one price, and selling it on to someone else at a higher price.
Unit Trust	Open-ended investment vehicle, structured under UK trust law. Priced using underlying NAV.
Yield	The income derivable from an investment, expressed as a percentage of the price of the investment.
Yield Gap	The difference between the yield on gilts and the yield on the UK index. Up until the 1960s, shares used to yield more than gilts because of their perceived greater risks. Since then, apart from occasional reappearances (12th March 2003), it has been the other way around because of the potential for dividends to grow, and the difference has been referred to as the 'Reverse yield gap'.

Acknowledgements & thanks

This book would not have been written without Jonathan Davis. Without his initial idea, subsequent encouragement (and gentle coercion!) together with his peerless editing skills the seed would not have borne fruit. I am extremely grateful to him. Similarly, the team at Harriman House, Myles Hunt, Tom Orchard and Nick Read has been excellent, although I am sure that Nick Read will be relieved not to be receiving any more phone calls from me! Many thanks to all of them.

There are many colleagues, past and present, to whom I am in debt. Many have given me chances where others would not have done. I have learnt from them all, and some have given me specific help during the writing of this book. From my days at Henderson I am very grateful to David Collingwood, Richard Eats, Jeremy Edwards, Richard Fellows, Richard Henderson, Giles Norman-Butler, Terry Williams and Ben Wrey. From my stint at Lazard, my thanks go to Robin Berrill, Victor Cazalet (now at Jupiter), Mike Chapman, Tom Cross-Brown, Herb Gullquist, Simon Hazlerigg, Christopher Melluish, Bob Morgenthau and Rupert Tyer. At Jupiter, specific thanks go to Edward Bonham Carter who allowed me to write as well as do the 'day job' and to the following people, both within and without the firm, who all helped in one way or another in putting this book together; Adrian Creedy, Gordon Davidson, Peter Hall, James Henderson, Colin Maloney, Tony Nutt, Martyn Page, Robert Parker, Sebastian Radcliffe, Mark Robinson, Max Usher, Tea Williamson and Alicia Wyllie.

I could not have completed the 'course' without the 100% support from my team of Peter Lawery, Lizzie Lee and Algy Smith-Maxwell. Without them, our success would not have been forthcoming and so this book would have never been written. I have been lucky enough to have worked with Pete and Algy for the last nine and seven years respectively, and I owe them a considerable debt of gratitude. Furthermore, I have learnt a lot from both of them. We have quite different characters but work well as a team, know what makes each other tick and have a bit of fun together as well. There is good chemistry, and God willing, we aim to remain as a team for a long time to come. Finally, Doone, Tom and Harry have been very patient whilst their husband/father has been engaged on this project, for which I am eternally grateful. I hope that it has all been worthwhile. Despite all the help I have received, any errors and omissions are, of course, my own.

John Chatfeild-Roberts
London
8th December 2005

Appendices

What is in the appendices

1. This Appendix gives further details of the style and performance of the main funds that I and my team run at Jupiter. It shows the fact sheets about each fund that we produce for distribution to clients, summarising the performance, ranking and holdings of each of the different portfolios. Note that the six funds each have different objectives and are managed accordingly.

    It is worth commenting on the fact that each portfolio contains between ten and fifteen funds and that some portfolios contain holdings of the same funds. This reflects the fact that a good fund can be put to more than one use. Even taking all the portfolios together, however, we need to find no more than 40 or so funds out of the 4,000 plus that are available. It really is a case of finding the best, and holding on to them until or unless market conditions change. More details about the track records of the individual funds that we own are given in Appendix Three.

2. This shows graphs of all the onshore UK index-tracking unit trusts and OEICs available to retail investors, that have been in existence for more than a year. Each graph is relative to the total return (i.e. dividend reinvested) version of the index the fund is trying to track, and is since the launch of the fund. Every single one of them underperforms its chosen index; some by more than others.

3. Appendix Three shows graphs of all the current holdings in the Jupiter Merlin Growth Portfolio Fund, discussed in Chapter Nine. Each graph is relative to the total return version of its relevant index.

1. Jupiter Merlin Portfolios, November 2005

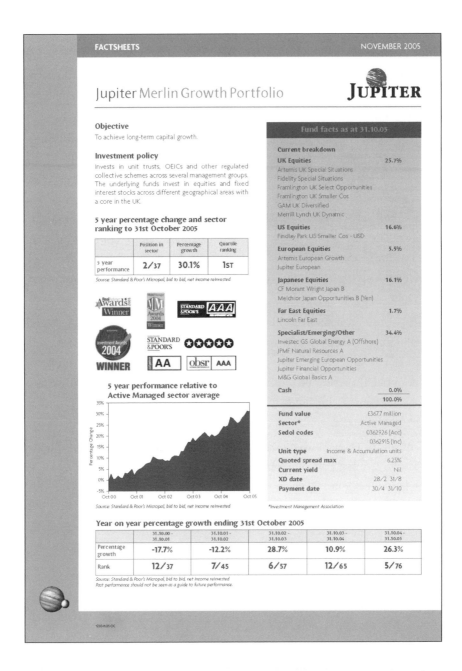

Jupiter Merlin Balanced Portfolio

JUPITER

Objective

To achieve long-term capital growth with income.

Investment policy

To invest in unit trusts, OEICs and other regulated collective schemes across several management groups. The underlying funds invest in international equities and fixed interest stocks.

3 year percentage change and sector ranking to 31st October 2005

	Position in sector	Percentage growth	Quartile ranking
Performance since launch***	6/83	59.1%	1ST

Source: Standard & Poor's Micropal, bid to bid, net income reinvested

STANDARD &POOR'S   AA

AA   obsr   AA

Performance since launch¹ relative to Balanced Managed sector average

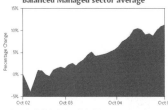

Source: Standard & Poor's Micropal, bid to bid, net income reinvested

Fund facts as at 31.10.05

Current breakdown

UK Equities	47.5%

Artemis Income
Framlington Monthly Income
INVESCO Perpetual Income
Jupiter Income
Jupiter UK Growth
Majedie UK Opportunities B

US Equities	6.2%

Findlay Park US Smaller Cos – USD

Japanese Equities	7.9%

JPM Japan
Melchior Japan Opportunities B (Yen)

Specialist/Emerging/Other	21.2%

Investec GS Global Energy A (Offshore)
Jupiter Emerging European Opportunities
Jupiter Financial Opportunities
M&G Global Basics A

Fixed Interest	13.7%

Royal London Sterling Extra Yield Bond Fund
Thames River High Income

Cash	3.5%
	100.0%

Fund value	£43.5 million
Sector*	Balanced Managed
Sedol codes	3184514 (Acc)
	3191075 (Inc)
Unit type	Income & Accumulation units
Quoted spread max	6.25%
Current yield	2.0%
XD date	31/5 30/11
Payment date	31/1 31/7

*Investment Management Association

Year on year percentage growth ending 31st October 2005¹

	31.10.02 - 31.10.03	31.10.03 - 31.10.04	31.10.04 - 31.10.05
Percentage growth	18.2%	11.5%	20.7%
Rank	14/83	7/96	4/102

Source: Standard & Poor's Micropal, bid to bid, net income reinvested
Past performance should not be seen as a guide to future performance.

¹The annual management charge and registration fee have increased from 01.09.05 by a total of approximately 1% pa. The performance would have been correspondingly reduced had the current fees applied since launch. On 01.09.05 the fund's objective changed to aim for growth with income as opposed to growth only, and this may also impact performance going forward.

1299.11.05 OC

Jupiter Merlin Income Portfolio

JUPITER

Objective
To achieve a high and rising income with some potential for capital growth.

Investment policy
Invests in unit trusts, OEICs and other regulated collective schemes across several management groups. The underlying funds invest in equities and fixed interest stocks, principally in the UK.

5 year percentage change and sector ranking to 31st October 2005

	Position in sector	Percentage growth	Quartile ranking
5 year performance	4/18	31.4%	1ST

Source: Standard & Poor's Micropal, bid to bid, net income reinvested

Fund facts as at 31.10.05

Current breakdown

UK Equities	54.3%

Artemis Income
Framlington Equity Income
Framlington Monthly Income
INVESCO Perpetual Income
Jupiter Income
Jupiter UK Growth
Rathbone Income

Other Equity	5.5%

Investec GS Global Energy A (Offshore)
Jupiter Emerging European Opportunities
Jupiter Japan Income

Fixed Interest	25.5%

Framlington Managed Income (ex High)
Old Mutual Corporate Bond
Royal London Sterling Extra Yield Bond Fund
Thames River High Income

Cash	14.7%
	100.0%

5 year performance relative to Cautious Managed sector average

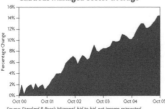

Source: Standard & Poor's Micropal, bid to bid, net income reinvested

Fund value	£360.8 million
Sector*	Cautious Managed
Sedol codes	0362937 (Acc)
	0362948 (Inc)
Unit type	Income & Accumulation units
Quoted spread max	6.25%
Current yield	3.42%
XD date	16/1 15/4 16/7 16/10
Payment date	15/3 15/6 15/9 15/12

*Investment Management Association

Year on year percentage growth ending 31st October 2005

	31.10.00 - 31.10.01	31.10.01 - 31.10.02	31.10.02 - 31.10.03	31.10.03 - 31.10.04	31.10.04 - 31.10.05
Percentage growth	-4.9%	-1.6%	11.8%	9.7%	14.5%
Rank	13/18	3/22	9/29	7/40	3/50

Source: Standard & Poor's Micropal, bid to bid, net income reinvested
Past performance should not be seen as a guide to future performance.

Jupiter Merlin Worldwide Portfolio

Objective
To achieve long-term capital growth.

Investment policy
Invests in unit trusts, OEICs and other regulated collective schemes across several management groups. The underlying funds invest in international equities and fixed interest stocks.

5 year percentage change and sector ranking to 31st October 2005

	Position in sector	Percentage growth	Quartile ranking
5 year performance	6/104	17.8%	1ST

Source: Standard & Poor's Micropal, bid to bid, net income reinvested

5 year performance relative to Global Growth sector average

Source: Standard & Poor's Micropal, bid to bid, net income reinvested

Fund facts as at 31.10.05

Current breakdown

UK Equities	7.5%
Majedie UK Opportunities B	
US Equities	20.2%
Findlay Park US Smaller Cos - USD	
Schroder US Smaller Cos Inc	
European Equities	9.6%
Artemis European Growth	
Jupiter European	
Japanese Equities	23.9%
CF Morant Wright Japan B	
JF Japan Alpha Plus S	
Melchior Japan Opportunities B (Yen)	
Far East Equities	2.1%
Lincoln Far East	
Specialist/Emerging/Other	35.1%
Investec Global Energy A (OEIC)	
JPMF Natural Resources A	
Jupiter Emerging European Opportunities	
Jupiter Financial Opportunities	
M&G Global Basics A	
Cash	1.6%
	100.0%

Fund value	£124.2 million
Sector*	Global Growth
Sedol codes	3166783 (Acc)
	0369983 (Inc)
Unit type	Income & Accumulation units
Quoted spread max	6.25%
Current yield	Nil
XD date	01/6
Payment date	31/7

*Investment Management Association

Year on year percentage growth ending 31st October 2005

	31.10.00 - 31.10.01	31.10.01 - 31.10.02	31.10.02 - 31.10.03	31.10.03 - 31.10.04	31.10.04 - 31.10.05
Percentage growth	-22.0%	-12.5%	21.5%	11.1%	27.8%
Rank	25/104	17/116	27/129	13/141	9/147

Source: Standard & Poor's Micropal, bid to bid, net income reinvested
Past performance should not be seen as a guide to future performance.

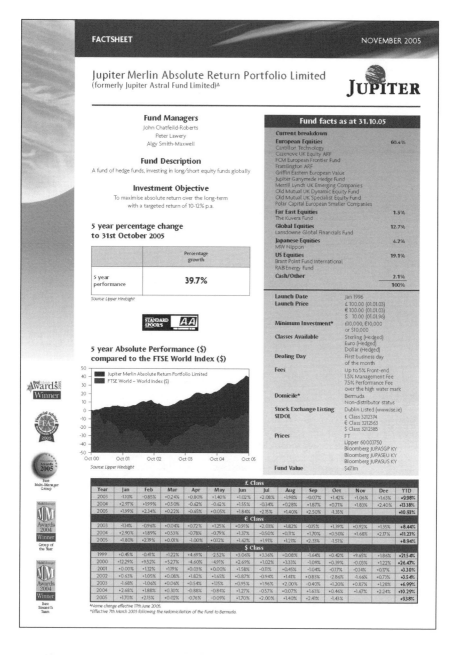

FACTSHEET

NOVEMBER 2005

Jupiter Merlin Absolute Return Portfolio Limited
(formerly Jupiter Astral Fund Limited)△

JUPITER

Fund Managers
John Chatfeild-Roberts
Peter Lawery
Algy Smith-Maxwell

Fund Description
A fund of hedge funds, investing in long/short equity funds globally

Investment Objective
To maximise absolute return over the long-term
with a targeted return of 10-12% p.a.

5 year percentage change
to 31st October 2005

	Percentage growth
5 year performance	**39.7%**

Source: Lipper Hindsight

STANDARD &POOR'S **AA**

5 year Absolute Performance ($)
compared to the FTSE World Index ($)

Jupiter Merlin Absolute Return Portfolio Limited
FTSE World – World Index ($)

Source: Lipper Hindsight

Fund facts as at 31.10.05

Current breakdown

European Equities	60.4%
Cantillon Technology	
Cazenove UK Equity ARF	
FCM European Frontier Fund	
Framlington ARF	
Griffin Eastern European Value	
Jupiter Ganymede Hedge Fund	
Merrill Lynch UK Emerging Companies	
Old Mutual UK Dynamic Equity Fund	
Old Mutual UK Specialist Equity Fund	
Polar Capital European Smaller Companies	
Far East Equities	1.5%
The Kuvera Fund	
Global Equities	12.7%
Lansdowne Global Financials Fund	
Japanese Equities	4.2%
MW Nippon	
US Equities	19.1%
Brant Point Fund International	
RAB Energy Fund	
Cash/Other	2.1%
	100%

Launch Date	Jan 1996
Launch Price	£ 100.00 (01.01.03)
	€ 100.00 (01.01.03)
	$ 10.00 (01.01.96)
Minimum Investment*	£10,000, €10,000 or $10,000
Classes Available	Sterling (Hedged) Euro (Hedged) Dollar (Hedged)
Dealing Day	First business day of the month
Fees	Up to 5% Front-end 1.5% Management Fee 7.5% Performance Fee over the high water mark
Domicile*	Bermuda Non-distributor status
Stock Exchange Listing SEDOL	Dublin Listed (www.ise.ie) £ Class 3212374 € Class 3212363 $ Class 3212385
Prices	FT Lipper 60003750 Bloomberg JUPASGP KY Bloomberg JUPASEU KY Bloomberg JUPASUS KY
Fund Value	$471.1m

£ Class

Year	Jan	Feb	Mar	Apr	May	Jun	Jul	Aug	Sep	Oct	Nov	Dec	YTD
2003	-1.10%	-0.85%	+0.24%	+0.80%	+1.40%	+1.02%	-2.08%	+1.98%	-0.07%	+1.42%	+1.06%	+1.63%	+9.98%
2004	+2.97%	+1.99%	+0.50%	-0.62%	-0.62%	+1.55%	-0.34%	+0.28%	+1.87%	+0.71%	+1.83%	+2.40%	+13.18%
2005	+1.99%	+2.34%	+0.22%	-0.65%	+0.05%	+1.84%	+2.15%	+1.40%	+2.50%	-1.35%			+10.93%

€ Class

Year	Jan	Feb	Mar	Apr	May	Jun	Jul	Aug	Sep	Oct	Nov	Dec	YTD
2003	-1.14%	-0.96%	+0.04%	+0.72%	+1.25%	+0.91%	-2.03%	+1.82%	-0.15%	+1.39%	+0.92%	+1.35%	+8.44%
2004	+2.90%	+1.85%	+0.53%	-0.78%	-0.79%	+1.37%	-0.50%	+0.11%	+1.70%	+0.50%	+1.68%	+2.17%	+11.23%
2005	+1.80%	+2.19%	+0.01%	-1.00%	+0.12%	+1.62%	+1.91%	+1.21%	+2.33%	-1.51%			+8.94%

$ Class

Year	Jan	Feb	Mar	Apr	May	Jun	Jul	Aug	Sep	Oct	Nov	Dec	YTD
1999	+0.45%	-0.41%	+1.22%	+4.69%	-2.52%	+3.06%	+3.36%	+0.08%	-1.64%	+0.42%	+9.65%	+1.86%	+21.54%
2000	+12.29%	+9.52%	+5.27%	-4.60%	-4.91%	+2.69%	+1.02%	+3.33%	-1.09%	+0.39%	-0.03%	+1.22%	+26.47%
2001	+0.00%	+1.32%	+1.39%	+0.03%	+0.00%	+1.58%	-0.11%	+0.45%	-1.04%	-0.37%	-0.14%	+0.17%	+3.30%
2002	+0.63%	+1.05%	+0.08%	+1.62%	+1.65%	+0.87%	-0.94%	+1.41%	+0.83%	-2.86%	-1.66%	+0.73%	+3.54%
2003	-1.68%	-1.06%	+0.06%	+0.54%	+1.35%	+0.95%	+1.96%	+2.00%	-0.40%	+1.20%	+0.87%	+1.28%	+6.99%
2004	+2.68%	+1.88%	+0.30%	-0.88%	-0.84%	+1.27%	-0.57%	+0.07%	+1.63%	+0.46%	+1.67%	+2.24%	+10.29%
2005	+1.70%	+2.13%	+0.02%	-0.76%	-0.09%	+1.70%	+2.00%	+1.40%	+2.41%	-1.43%			+9.38%

△Name change effective 17th June 2005.
*Effective 7th March 2005 following the redomiciliation of the Fund to Bermuda.

Jupiter Offshore Portfolio Fund Limited

Fund Managers
John Chatfeild-Roberts
Peter Lawery
Algy Smith-Maxwell

Fund Description
A fund of funds, investing in long only mutual funds, with some exposure to investment trusts and long/short equity funds (limited to 20%) globally.

Investment Objective
To maximise long-term total return, in excess of the FTSE World Index (£).

5 year percentage change and sector ranking to 31st October 2005

	Position in sector	Percentage growth	Quartile ranking
5 year performance	19/596	+36.0%	1ST

Source: Lipper Hindsight
Sector: Lipper Global, Equity Global

Performance relative to FTSE World Index (£)

Source: Lipper Hindsight

Fund facts as at 31.10.05

Current breakdown

UK Equities	15.7%
Framlington Absolute Return UK	
Majedie UK Opportunities	
Marlborough Slater Recovery	
US Equities	27.8%
Brant Point Fund International	
Findlay Park US Smaller Companies USD	
Schroder US Smaller Companies	
European Equities	7.1%
Argos Argonaut	
Japanese Equities	15.7%
CF Morant Wright Japan B	
Melchior Japan Opportunities	
Specialist/Emerging/Other	33.0%
Investec GSF Global Energy	
JPMF Natural Resources A	
Jupiter Emerging European Opportunities	
Jupiter Financial Opportunities	
RAB Energy Fund	
Cash	0.7%
	100.0%

Minimum Investment	£10,000
Dealing	Daily
Base Currency	Sterling
Fees	5% initial fee, 1.25% annual management fee, 7.5% performance fee of excess performance over FTSE World Index (£)
Domicile	Jersey, Non Distributor Status
Stock Exchange Listing	Channel Islands Stock Exchange
Prices	Financial Times Lipper 60003751 Bloomberg JUPOFGW KY
Sedol	0508236

Fund Value	£19.40m
Original Launch Price	£10.00
Original Launch Date	January 1988
Bid Price (31.10.05)	£53.749

Growth Class

Year	Jan	Feb	Mar	Apr	May	Jun	Jul	Aug	Sep	Oct	Nov	Dec	YTD
1999	+0.76%	+3.73%	+1.23%	+4.52%	-2.43%	+2.67%	-0.17%	+2.06%	-4.97%	+0.21%	+10.55%	+0.93%	+19.91%
2000	+4.87%	+7.72%	+3.22%	-2.55%	+1.31%	+1.73%	+1.57%	+6.89%	-2.36%	+0.71%	-0.18%	-1.62%	+22.77%
2001	+3.19%	-0.77%	-4.40%	+4.21%	+3.23%	-2.91%	-3.45%	-0.42%	-13.44%	+3.91%	+5.45%	+1.11%	-5.74%
2002	-1.72%	+0.64%	+2.77%	+0.59%	+2.95%	-4.62%	-10.90%	+1.46%	-5.21%	+0.70%	+3.42%	-3.54%	-13.05%
2003	-2.59%	+0.42%	+1.53%	+4.79%	+4.04%	+1.72%	+5.46%	+5.46%	-2.45%	+3.23%	+0.33%	+2.61%	+26.01%
2004	+2.75%	+0.63%	+2.22%	-2.09%	-5.95%	+3.05%	-2.24%	+0.90%	+2.34%	+2.64%	+3.80%	+0.65%	+13.20%
2005	+2.38%	+4.42%	-0.80%	-2.38%	+1.54%	+3.16%	+6.01%	+1.67%	+6.41%	-4.76%			+18.45%

2. Graphs of all the index-tracking unit trusts and OEICs

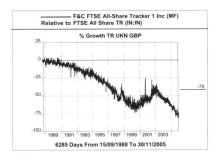

F&C FTSE All-Share Tracker 1 Inc (MF)
Relative to FTSE All Share TR (IN:IN)

% Growth TR UKN GBP

6285 Days From 15/09/1988 To 30/11/2005

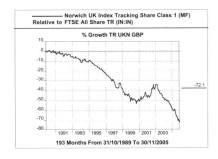

Norwich UK Index Tracking Share Class 1 (MF)
Relative to FTSE All Share TR (IN:IN)

% Growth TR UKN GBP

193 Months From 31/10/1989 To 30/11/2005

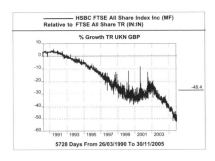

HSBC FTSE All Share Index Inc (MF)
Relative to FTSE All Share TR (IN:IN)

% Growth TR UKN GBP

5728 Days From 26/03/1990 To 30/11/2005

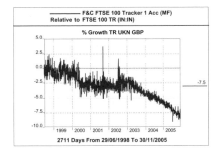

F&C FTSE 100 Tracker 1 Acc (MF)
Relative to FTSE 100 TR (IN:IN)

% Growth TR UKN GBP

2711 Days From 29/06/1998 To 30/11/2005

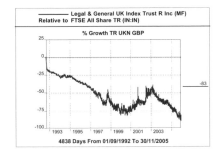

Legal & General UK Index Trust R Inc (MF)
Relative to FTSE All Share TR (IN:IN)

% Growth TR UKN GBP

4838 Days From 01/09/1992 To 30/11/2005

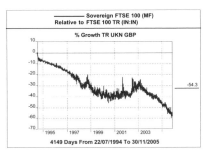

Sovereign FTSE 100 (MF)
Relative to FTSE 100 TR (IN:IN)

% Growth TR UKN GBP

4149 Days From 22/07/1994 To 30/11/2005

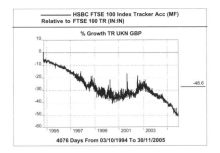

HSBC FTSE 100 Index Tracker Acc (MF)
Relative to FTSE 100 TR (IN:IN)

% Growth TR UKN GBP

4076 Days From 03/10/1994 To 30/11/2005

Virgin UK Index Tracking Trust (MF)
Relative to FTSE All Share TR (IN:IN)

% Growth TR UKN GBP

3925 Days From 03/03/1995 To 30/11/2005

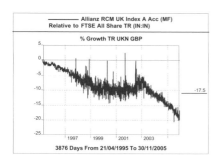

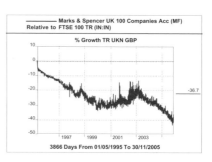

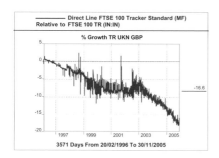

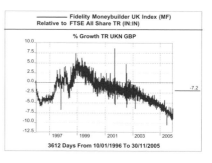

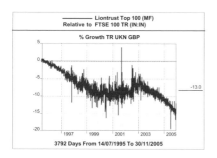

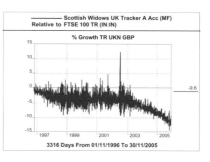

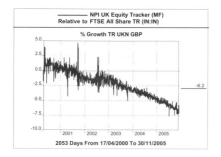

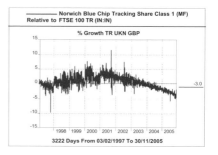

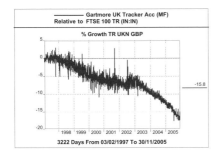

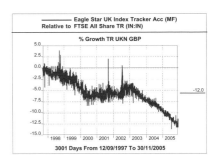

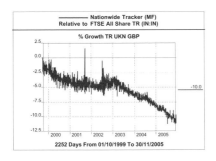

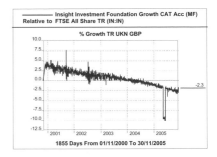

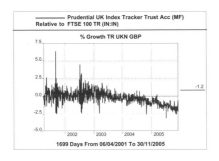

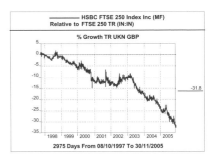

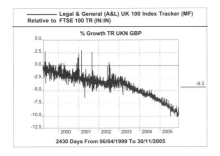

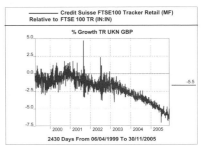

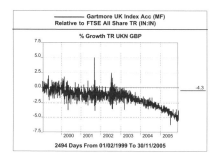

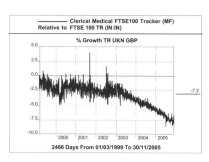

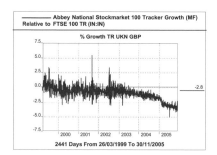

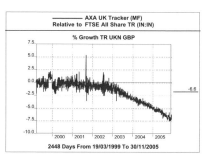

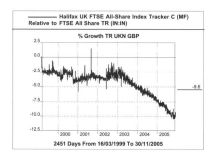

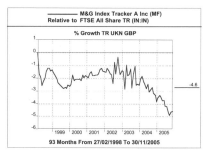

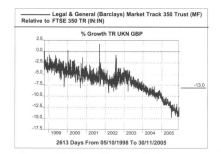

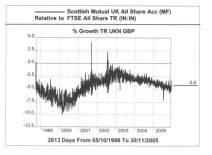

Source of all graphs: Lipper, total return, GBP, since launch at the beginning of the fixed-price offer period, relative to their respective index, to 30th November 2005.

N.B.   The figure quoted on the right hand side of each graph shows the amount by which each fund has underperformed its benchmark index since launch.   For example, the St. James's Place Fund above returned 5.6% over the period versus 13.2% for the index, underperformance of 7.6% (13.2% minus 5.6%).

3. All Jupiter Merlin Growth Portfolio Fund Holdings

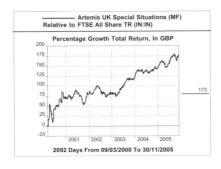

Artemis UK Special Situations (MF)
Relative to FTSE All Share TR (IN:IN)
Percentage Growth Total Return, In GBP
173
2092 Days From 09/03/2000 To 30/11/2005

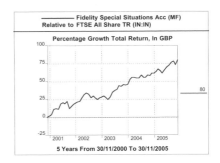

Fidelity Special Situations Acc (MF)
Relative to FTSE All Share TR (IN:IN)
Percentage Growth Total Return, In GBP
80
5 Years From 30/11/2000 To 30/11/2005

Framlington UK Smaller Companies Inc (MF)
Relative to FTSE Small Cap (X It) TR (IN:IN)
Percentage Growth Total Return, In GBP
76
1678 Days From 27/04/2001 To 30/11/2005

Framlington UK Select Opportunities (MF)
Relative to FTSE All Share TR (IN)
% Growth TR UKN GBP
27.7
39 Months From 30/08/2002 To 30/11/2005

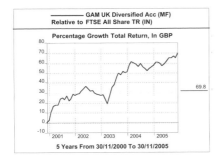

GAM UK Diversified Acc (MF)
Relative to FTSE All Share TR (IN)
Percentage Growth Total Return, In GBP
69.8
5 Years From 30/11/2000 To 30/11/2005

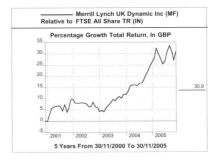

Merrill Lynch UK Dynamic Inc (MF)
Relative to FTSE All Share TR (IN)
Percentage Growth Total Return, In GBP
30.9
5 Years From 30/11/2000 To 30/11/2005

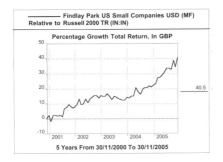

Findlay Park US Small Companies USD (MF)
Relative to Russell 2000 TR (IN:IN)
Percentage Growth Total Return, In GBP
40.5
5 Years From 30/11/2000 To 30/11/2005

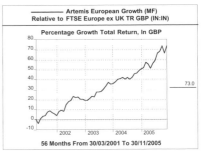

Artemis European Growth (MF)
Relative to FTSE Europe ex UK TR GBP (IN:IN)
Percentage Growth Total Return, In GBP
73.0
56 Months From 30/03/2001 To 30/11/2005

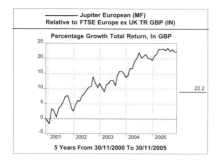

Jupiter European (MF)
Relative to FTSE Europe ex UK TR GBP (IN)
Percentage Growth Total Return, In GBP
22.2
5 Years From 30/11/2000 To 30/11/2005

CF Morant Wright Japan B Acc (MF)
Relative to Topix TR (IN:IN)
Percentage Growth Total Return, In GBP
14.5
933 Days From 12/05/2003 To 30/11/2005

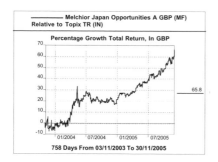

Melchior Japan Opportunities A GBP (MF)
Relative to Topix TR (IN)
Percentage Growth Total Return, In GBP
65.8
758 Days From 03/11/2003 To 30/11/2005

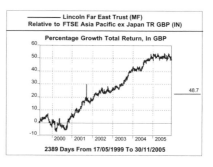

Lincoln Far East Trust (MF)
Relative to FTSE Asia Pacific ex Japan TR GBP (IN)
Percentage Growth Total Return, In GBP
48.7
2389 Days From 17/05/1999 To 30/11/2005

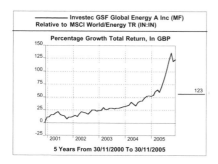

Investec GSF Global Energy A Inc (MF)
Relative to MSCI World/Energy TR (IN:IN)
Percentage Growth Total Return, In GBP
123
5 Years From 30/11/2000 To 30/11/2005

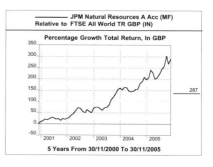

JPM Natural Resources A Acc (MF)
Relative to FTSE All World TR GBP (IN)
Percentage Growth Total Return, In GBP
287
5 Years From 30/11/2000 To 30/11/2005

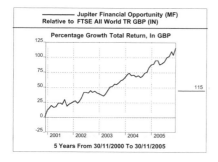

Jupiter Financial Opportunity (MF)
Relative to FTSE All World TR GBP (IN)
Percentage Growth Total Return, In GBP
115
5 Years From 30/11/2000 To 30/11/2005

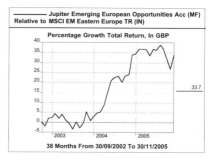

Jupiter Emerging European Opportunities Acc (MF)
Relative to MSCI EM Eastern Europe TR (IN)
Percentage Growth Total Return, In GBP
33.7
38 Months From 30/09/2002 To 30/11/2005

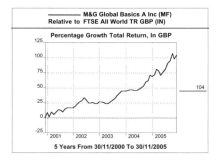

Source of all graphs: Lipper, total return, GBP, 5 years or since launch, relative their benchmark index, to 30th November 2005

Index